The Baroness, *the* Mogul,
and the Forgotten History
of the
First Guggenheim Museum

Museum of Non-Objective Painting, 24 East 54 St., N.Y., 1939.

The Baroness, *the* Mogul, *and the* Forgotten History *of the* First Guggenheim Museum

— *as told by one who was there* —

Rolph Scarlett

in collaboration with
Harriet Tannin

2004
To our dear friends, Trudy and Herb,
with love, Harriet

Midmarch Arts Press

New York

Library of Congress Catalog Card Number 2002113699
ISBN 1-877675-38-5

Copyright © 2003 Harriet Tannin and Midmarch Arts Press,
Bearsville and New York City, New York
All rights reserved

No part of the contents of this book covered by copyright herein
may be reproduced or used in any form or by any means — including
photocopying, recording, taping, or information retrieval systems —
without the written permission of the publisher.

Printed in the United States of America

Published in 2003 by
Midmarch Arts Press
New York, NY 10025

Acknowledgments

The creation of this book of Rolph Scarlett's memoirs was long and arduous and required the assistance of many people. Beginning in 1980 Rolph and I began to edit and enlarge upon a rough draft of a book that he had begun writing years earlier. Over the years this was followed by frequent interviews with Scarlett which resulted in additional changes.

I am indebted to Dr. William Finn, former Dean of Fine and Performing Arts at the State University of New York at New Paltz, for his interest and for providing letters of introduction to the staff at the Solomon R. Guggenheim Museum in New York, who made the facilities and research departments of the museum available to me. My special thanks to Louise Averill Svendsen, Ward Jackson, Vivian Endicott Barnett, and Joan Lukach—the information gained from them was invaluable.

Thanks are due to Tom Hull and Richard Ciganko who videotaped my interviews of Rolph Scarlett providing important documentation in Scarlett's own words.

Thanks also to Donna Rogers who spent many hours assisting me in organizing and editing the manuscript, as did Elizabeth Pollet, Scarlett's stepdaughter, who supported me since the beginning of this project.

I am indebted to my publisher Cynthia Navaretta of Midmarch Arts Press. Without her interest, knowledge, talent, and research the manuscript would never have reached its final state. And to Kari Grimsby who contributed invaluable support to the final book.

Finally—this project could never have been completed without the understanding, love, and constant support of my husband Albert.

—H.T.

Contents

Prologue • ix
Foreword, *by Harriet Tannin* • xi
Preface, *by Rolph Scarlett* • xv

Chapter I • 1
The Museum of Non-objective Painting, 1939
First Exhibition of the Solomon R. Guggenheim Collection, 1936

Chapter II • 7
Plans for a Target-Guided Missile
Meeting Hilla Rebay

Chapter III • 13
Childhood and Youth: Guelph and New York

Chapter IV • 21
Trip to Switzerland and Meeting Paul Klee
Years in Ohio and Recognition as a Non-objective Painter
Move to California in mid-1920s and Working in the Movie Industry
Designing Sets at the Pasadena Playhouse and Exhibiting in California
Return to Canada at the Beginning of the Depression and Settling in New York in 1933

Chapter V • 28
Lecturing at The Museum of Non-objective Painting
Rudolph Bauer's Arrival in America

Chapter VI • 35
The World of Non-objective Art
Bauer's Pre-eminence

Chapter VII • 44
Rebay's Day in Court

Chapter VIII • 49
A Visit to Green Farms
Rebay's Vision for the Ideal Museum
An Offer to become Co-Director of the Museum

Chapter IX • 56
Hilla Rebay's Stature as Artist and Visionary
Acquiring Piet Mondrian's Paintings on the Day of His Funeral

Chapter X • 61
Frank Lloyd Wright and the Guggenheim Museum

CHAPTER XI • 68
The Flim-Flam Man and Ralph Albert Blakelock

CHAPTER XII • 73
Some Thoughts on the Difficulties Between an Artist's Legacy
(Paul Gaugin) and an Affluent Family

CHAPTER XIII • 76
So-Called Art Critics—Clement Greenberg and Irving Sandler
Peggy Guggenheim
Exhibiting in the Whitney Museum, 1951
Non-objective vs. Abstract Expressionism

CHAPTER XIV • 84
Tribute to Baroness Hilla von Rebay:
Guggenheim Museum Exhibition, 1968

CHAPTER XV • 91
Rudolf Bauer Exhibition, New York, 1970
and How the Non-objective Movement Was Wiped Out

CHAPTER XVI • 93
Homage to Hilla Rebay, Exhibition,
Carlson Gallery, University of Bridgeport, 1972
Disposition of Rebay's Estate

CHAPTER XVII • 97
Summing Up: "Skunkses is Skunkses"

EPILOGUE • 100
Meeting Lyonel Feininger
Hilla Rebay and Solomon R. Guggenheim

CHRONOLOGY • 105

ABOUT HARRIET TANNIN • 109

COLOR PLATES • 111

APPENDIX
Letters of Rolph Scarlett and Hilla Rebay • 119
Letters and Descriptions of Scarlett's Missile Design • 132
Newspaper Clippings and Catalogue Essay • 144

Credits • 150

Prologue

Memory is the most paradoxical of the senses . . . at the same time so powerful that even the most fleeting impressions can be stored, forgotten completely, and then reproduced in perfect detail years later, and yet so unreliable that it can play us completely false.

— Peter Freund
neuropsychiatrist at the Institute of Psychiatry, London

As you will read in the Foreword and Preface, this is the story of four people as told by one of them, Rolph Scarlett, an artist befriended and supported by the other three — Baroness Hilla Rebay von Ehrenwiesen, director of the Museum of Non-objective Painting from 1939 to 1952; Solomon R. Guggenheim, art collector and financial supporter of the museum; and Rudolf Bauer, represented by 350 paintings in the museum's collection.

The Museum of Non-objective Painting was the earliest incarnation of the now-famous Solomon R. Guggenheim "global museum."

However, a large part of the story involves many other off-stage participants such as:

Frank Lloyd Wright, architect of the building he described as "the sovereignty of the individual."

James Johnson Sweeney, who succeeded Rebay in the early 1950s as director of the Guggenheim Museum.

Thomas Messer, who followed Sweeney as director and whose name only appears in quotations from a catalogue essay.

Irene Guggenheim, Solomon's wife, who is never mentioned in Scarlett's stories, yet is the linchpin of his wrath. Irene had regularly accompanied Solomon on his art buying trips to Europe in the late '20s and early '30s, until his liaison with Rebay became too public to ignore. From then on she discreetly withdrew from active participation in Solomon's social life and focused her interests on charitable work. It is revenge for her "pain and suffering" that her relatives on the Board sought in expunging Rebay and her artists from the museum.

Solomon Guggenheim's daughters, two of whom (Eleanor, Countess Castle Stewart, and Barbara, Mrs. Fred Wettach), served as trustees on the Foundation's Board.

Lord Castle Stewart, husband of Solomon Guggenheim's daughter, Eleanor, and head of the Guggenheim Non-objective Foundation in the late 1940s.

Harry F. Guggenheim, nephew of Solomon and president of the Foundation supporting the museum from 1957 to 1969.

Peggy Guggenheim, niece of Solomon, art patron and avid collector.

Clement Greenberg, art critic and early supporter of the abstract-expressionist artists, and a host of others including poet Delmore Schwartz, who introduced Scarlett to Greenberg.

Vasily Kandinsky, with 140 paintings (number varies from 180 to 130 after 50 were sold at auction in 1964) in the museum's collection.

Artists *Jackson Pollock, Piet Mondrian, Ralph Albert Blakelock*, and *Paul Gauguin.*

All figure in Scarlett's reminiscences.

His story starts with what Scarlett remembers as the best years of his life — his recognition as a non-objective painter by those who set the standard for the style. He then weaves back and forth, exploring his memories of earlier successes and retelling anecdotes that are still vividly remembered. He freely vents his disappointments. Although some of his stories are devastatingly true, he may at times be a flawed and biased observer, but makes a valuable contribution for the light he sheds on a formative period in art that was very vital in its day and provides a record of actual history with local color and human interest. As we know, memories grow dim over time and it is not easy to reconstruct a life or an era. Our supportive research of other writings of the period in an attempt to verify Scarlett's sometimes harsh criticism, found vast discrepancies and a murky record of the time since everyone personalizes history as he or she remembers it. We have in those instances inserted an observer's voice, in italics, where documented material differs from Scarlett's story. And although some of his stories may strain the reader's credulity, the most fantastic of them are supported by documentation such as letters and newspaper clippings. We can accept his total recall of conversations that took place some forty years earlier by understanding that he had probably reviewed them in his mind again and again over the years. They were, after all, the major events in his life.

In the Appendix there are several letters addressed to Scarlett from Hilla Rebay from 1939 through 1951 that indicate her deteriorating relationship with Scarlett who was no longer doing things "her way." However, Scarlett remained steadfast in his admiration and devotion to the Baroness, Solomon Guggenheim, and Rudolf Bauer. Scarlett's devotion is closely matched by artist Harriet Tannin's twelve years spent inteviewing and taping his stories.

— *CN*, 2002

Foreword

When Solomon Guggenheim died on November 3, 1949, his museum, conceived as a temple for his collection of non-objective art, had been in existence for about ten years. Hilla Rebay (1890-1967) was its high priestess. The Russian Vasily Kandinsky (1866-1944) was its major artist. He had pioneered non-objective painting and 140 of his works were in the permanent collection. Rudolf Bauer (1889-1953), his German counterpart, was represented by 350 paintings; the American Rolph Scarlett (1889-1984) was represented by 70 paintings. These works by Kandinsky, Bauer, and Scarlett had been on permanent exhibition at the original Guggenheim Museum [Museum of Non-objective Painting] on East 54th Street. In 1943, Guggenheim had engaged Frank Lloyd Wright to create a monumental new museum on Fifth Avenue to enshrine his collection for the world to enjoy. But it didn't happen as planned.

In 1970 I became a student of Rolph Scarlett, who was then living in Woodstock, New York, not far from my studio. I had come across a bottle of poppy oil while shopping at a local art supply store. When I asked about it, I learned that it was kept in stock just for Rolph Scarlett, the painter. That was the first time I had heard the name of Rolph Scarlett, who was to become so important a factor in my life. The clerk did not know what he did with poppy oil, but assured me that if I telephoned, the garrulous eighty-year-old artist would tell me all about it.

I telephoned from the store immediately, and Rolph said, "Do you have a minute? Come over and I'll tell you about it."

The drive to his studio was short, but the minute lasted four hours. Anyone who has met Rolph has enjoyed the same experience. "Did you ever hear of the Guggenheim Museum?" he asked. The answer of course was yes. "Well," he continued, "they have sixty or seventy of my paintings, Non-objective paintings bought for their permanent collection, but can you see them? No. They are buried because the Guggenheim family hated Hilla Rebay. And do you know why they hated Rebay? No, of course you don't. Nobody does. I am the only one still alive who knows what really happened. Hilla Rebay is dead. Solomon Guggenheim is dead. Rudolf Bauer is dead. When I tell the real story, the lid will blow off the pot. It is a scandal. The Guggenheim family will try to stop me, but they will never buy me off. Not for a million dollars. I'll never forgive them for trying to kill non-objective painting. They buried my paintings and Bauer's too. Don't try to telephone the Guggenheim and ask to see my paintings. They'll never show them to you." Suddenly he asked, "Am I boring you? Do you want me to stop?

I listened to Scarlett at least once a week for twelve years. He was a marvelous storyteller. He would not let me leave. His stories of the real history of art of the 1930s, '40s and '50s are not to be found in any of the books. After listening to Rolph, I would try to read about him and the museum. Many who heard his stories tried to find some documentation, but all failed. One had to wonder if the Guggenheim family, as Rolph claimed, really could kill off a whole art movement or if Rolph's stories were the delusional ramblings of an old man.

This remarkable man, the last survivor of an early era of American modernist art, was disappearing from history, perhaps due to simple neglect, perhaps by design. His scrapbook was incomplete and his most important works were sequestered from public view in the storerooms of the Guggenheim Museum. If there were ever to be a resurgence of interest in American non-objective painting, Rolph's works represented one of its critical dimensions. And even if there were no such resurgence, future students and historians of art should have access to the work.

In 1979, when Rolph was ninety, I asked him if he would like me to make a videotape of him telling his stories so as to preserve their accuracy and flavor. He was pleased. Then I asked if he would like me to photograph his paintings and try to find a gallery in New York City for a one-man show. That pleased him even more. Then I asked if he would like me to put the stories he had told me so often into a book. He himself had started a book, writing in two spiral-bound notebooks in the 1960s, covering the years of his personal involvement with the Guggenheim Museum. It ranged from 1938 when Hilla Rebay and Solomon Guggenheim bought one of his paintings for their planned museum. It ended about eleven years later with the death of Solomon Guggenheim, which turned out to be the end of the Museum of Non-objective Painting. His title for the book was "Skunkses Is Skunkses," Hilla Rebay's phrase of contempt for those who fought her plans to advance non-objective art. The prospect had both Rolph and me laughing. A videotape. A one-man show. A book of his memoirs. It sounded like a TV script for "Fantasy Island."

The videotape "Who Is Rolph Scarlett?" was completed in 1980. Along the way, I interviewed R. Louise Averill Svendsen, then senior curator of the Guggenheim Museum. She was charming and helpful. We spent about two and a half-hours exchanging information. Finally I asked about Rolph's paintings, and if there was any hope they would ever hang on the Guggenheim Museum walls again. She was not very encouraging. I then asked if it would be possible for the museum to lend Rolph's paintings for a gallery show. She agreed.

Then Rolph suddenly became very ill and confined to his bed. With the help of the tape I was able to organize, restore, and photograph many of his paintings. I used the videotape to reintroduce Rolph to various New York City galleries. In 1982 the Washburn Gallery in New York showed forty of Rolph's paintings from the 1940s. The Guggenheim Museum, as Dr. Svendsen had promised, contributed three of his large oils. This exhibit was followed by a second one-man show at the Washburn Gallery in 1983.

When I heard in 1982 that Dr. John Lane, director of the Museum of Art, Carnegie Institute in Pittsburgh was curating an exhibit of "Abstract Painting and Sculpture in America: 1927-1944" I suggested including some of Rolph's paintings in the exhibit. Remembering the 1940s and Scarlett's role as one of the most important American non-objective painters, Lane was delighted. When the exhibit opened on November 5, 1983, two of Rolph's oils were included. The exhibit traveled to the San Francisco Museum of Modern Art, The Minneapolis Institute of Art, and the Whitney Museum of American Art.

My last promise to Rolph was to finish his book of memoirs called "Skunkses is Skunkses," now renamed *The Baroness, the Mogul, and the Forgotten History of the First Guggenheim Museum*. This book was about the origin of Non-objective art in the United States and the building of the Museum of Non-objective Painting through the efforts of Solomon R. Guggenheim and Hilla Rebay. It starts with the museum's opening in 1939 with Rolph Scarlett the only American included. The story of Guggenheim's purchase of more than 100 of Scarlett's paintings for the museum and his own personal collection when Scarlett was the only American painter exhibiting regularly with Kandinsky and Rudolf Bauer is here. Scarlett felt it was his duty to let the world know the true story.

Before he died in 1984 he had the pleasure of hearing every chapter, which he did with great glee, and edited exactly to his wishes. The stories you are about to read are the same ones I heard again and again, and never tired of no matter how many times.

When Rolph died my promises to him had been fulfilled: the interview on videotape, solo exhibitions in New York City, museum shows, and a finished manuscript of his memoirs from our interviews over a five-year period. Even unpublished they have already been a resource to museums and historians. The Guggenheim Museum let me borrow six Scarlett paintings for a retrospective I curated in Woodstock, New York, in 1993. Once more, in 1996, a Scarlett painting was taken from storage to hang in the Guggenheim Museum's exhibit "Abstraction in the Twentieth Century." In

2000 another painting was taken out of storage and loaned to the Whitney Museum of American Art for the exhibit, "A Century of Art." A new generation of viewers has now seen his paintings from the 1930s and 1940s.

— *Harriet Tannin, 2000*

In the mid-1990s the Guggenheim Museum deaccessioned paintings by Scarlett, Bauer, and Rebay through a private dealer and a New York gallery. See The New York Times, *May 3, 1996, article in Appendix.*

Preface

The creation of art reflects the intellectual and spiritual development of mankind. The recording of creative efforts helps insure their perpetuation. I don't think anybody knows the real history of the Non-objective movement in this country.like I do, because nobody else who was part of it is still alive.

As I approach the end of my life, over half of which has been devoted to non-objective painting, I realize that much of what should have been recorded as an important part of this country's art history has not been. Solomon R. Guggenheim and Hilla Rebay established the Museum of Non-objective Painting in connection with a Foundation to show the new art, its artists, and to educate the public. But I am the only living witness to many of the events surrounding non-objective art.

The whole story, the Guggenheim Collection, the early museum, the present museum, how things were manipulated after Solomon died, ought to be cleared up, at least insofar as it can be. But this one died, that one died, the next one died; there is no one left who knows, so now it's back in my lap.

Vasily Kandinsky first coined the phrase "non-objective art" in Germany in 1910. The term is self-explanatory. Non-objective means without an object. Previously all painting of all kinds in every part of the world was based on a real, existing, three-dimensional object. Whether a person, a tree, a building, the sea, a landscape, or a bowl of fruit, the object was the focus.

With the invention of the camera the possibility of reproducing the subject-matter with near-perfect realism became a reality. Although the camera could reproduce the objective world and originally served as a copying device, artists, including photographers, began to search for new horizons. Many of the early *isms* in modern art concerned themselves with some kind of distortion of the object. A table might be viewed from top or bottom and depicted as it might appear from various angles. The same with persons, landscapes or any other parts of reality. But, and it's a big but, the object was still there in some form.

Non-objective art rejected the external world as subject matter. Thus the drastic departure from *copying* to *creating*. Non-objective art is pure creation!

This drastic departure is barely mentioned in American art history.

Non-objective art is amply covered in world histories of modern art with its origin attributed to the German group the Blaue Reiter of which Kandinsky was a co-leader.

That it may have been deliberately omitted is scandalous. Reality, as we perceive it, is fleeting. Peoples, cities, countries, whole civilizations pass away. But ideas endure. Ideas warrant our protection and our reverence, whether or not we agree with them. Ideas are the essential record of humanity.

The Non-objective Museum in 1939 and the Foundation in 1937 were established to promote non-objective art and art education in America. But the project was redirected after the death of Solomon Guggenheim and the policy changes that followed.

When Mr. Guggenheim originally sponsored the new museum, he was thunderstruck at the response — not only of the public, but painters from all over the country wrote requesting catalogues and reproductions. Within a year of the opening non-objective paintings were being submitted to the museum and Hilla Rebay and I agreed that there was enough new and exciting work to organize an exhibition.

Space was tight. The main floor was filled with Kandinskys and Bauers. The second floor too had mostly European non-objective artists with established reputations, some of them recent arrivals in America. I suggested that the mezzanine balcony be used and it was.

Perhaps because the war was on [in Germany] and Rebay was German (she later became an American citizen) and so many of the works shown were by German artists, the New York critics had at first been niggardly with praise. But lo and behold! the new American work was eventually reviewed favorably!

This show was only the beginning. The exhibits of new American non-objective work continued for ten years, even after the museum moved to its temporary quarters on Fifth Avenue. [A residential building at 1071, which was torn down in 1951 when the entire block front from 88th to 89th Streets was secured for the construction of the present museum.]

I always regretted that Kandinsky's term "non-objective," has been ignored in favor of "abstract expressionism," which was the term originally used in Germany for the new work. The artists of the New York School, the most famous of whom was Jackson Pollock, also called themselves abstract expressionists. And their spokesman, the critic Clement Greenberg, used the term widely and made it famous.

"Expressionism" was widely used to describe the work of Kandinsky and occasionally "abstract" but rarely a combination of the two.

I am an artist. Not a writer. Not an historian. But I lived and worked through those fascinating times and I was intimately involved with the people who shaped those events.

You may find my tales interesting. Or you may not.

— Rolph Scarlett, 1980

ART OF TOMORROW

RUDOLF BAUER

FIFTH CATALOGUE OF THE SOLOMON R. GUGGENHEIM
COLLECTION OF NON-OBJECTIVE PAINTINGS
PART OF WHICH IS TEMPORARILY EXHIBITED
AT 24 EAST 54TH STREET, NEW YORK CITY
OPENING JUNE 1ST, 1939

SOLOMON R. GUGGENHEIM FOUNDATION
NEW YORK

Chapter I

The Museum of Non-objective Painting, 1939

An event of June, 1939, at 24 East 54th Street in New York City, is still being felt around the world of the arts. I mean the opening of the Guggenheim Non-objective Museum with a show titled "The Art of Tomorrow." The attending crowd may have had no inkling of the flaming torch so casually flung into the tinderbox of creative energy in this country, and of the sparks soon to be scattered all over the world.

Even now, so many years later, I marvel at the diminutive structure of this unobtrusive opening, the casualness of the visitors, and the almost childish indifference of the critics and reporters who covered the opening.

What an entertaining beast it has turned out to be. Even after all these years this creature seems to be as vigorous and unpredictable as ever, and it gives promise of being alive and kicking for a long time to come.

I was an invited guest that memorable night with one of my paintings hanging there. Then, another opening, years later, was an outgrowth of this one, the opening of the Frank Lloyd Wright building, the Solomon R. Guggenheim Museum, which replaced the original. However, this second opening, as far as I can see, had not the least importance to the art world. In fact, if it had never happened it would not have made the slightest difference to the growth and importance of our cultural life as expressed in painting and sculpture.

In sum, the original small and rather retiring little museum set the art world on fire, while the present Guggenheim Museum which replaced it has turned out to have practically no influence at all except for its interest as a unique building and the so-called worst museum ever built does not deter the public from streaming in. They come to see the remarkable building, not the "art" it houses.

This distorted view growing out of Scarlett's disappointment at the disappearance of his works from the original museum's collection is far from an accurate assessment of the importance and impact of the Museum. Its permanent collection is highly regarded and the building is acknowledged as the precucurser of our present golden age of museum architecture. At this time, in 2002, the Guggenheim has a worldwide reputation as a global museum model with locations in New York (Guggenheim Soho closed late-2001 but a Frank D. Gehry designed building is to be built on the waterfront of the East River in Lower Manhattan); Venice; Berlin; Bilbao, Spain; Las Vegas (two, the Jewel Box and the Big Box, designed by Rem Koolhaas) plus more to come in South America; and additional relationships with several major partner institutions around the world such as the State Hermitage Museum in St.

Petersburg, Russia, the Kunsthistoriches Museum in Vienna, and the Galleria Gottardo in Lugano, Switzerland..

Solomon Guggenheim and Hilla Rebay had worried about the future, often discussing their fears with me. They realized that after Sol's death, with his influence and support absent and the considerable influence of his heirs brought into play, the project might be abandoned. He felt strongly that art should not be simply a plaything for an affluent family or, for that matter, be used to glorify one affluent man. This is why he wanted the museum called the Museum of Non-objective Art or something of that sort, not the Solomon R. Guggenheim Memorial Museum.

At times, when I met Guggenheim for lunch, I found him in a state of considerable agitation. He would say, "I think I'll turn the collection over to Columbia University."

"If you really care about non-objective art, don't put it there, they'll kill it."

Maybe six months later he would say, "Well, I've been dealing with the Modern Museum and I think I'll give it to them."

"Don't do that, they'll kill it even faster than Columbia." The problem at that particular moment was that no dealers wanted it, no critic wanted it, the public didn't want it yet. What was he going to do with it?

The non-objective movement had finally become his whole life. He wanted the collection, the Foundation, and the museum to be preserved as originally conceived.

Yet, what he feared did happen. Soon after Solomon Guggenheim's death, the museum's name was changed to the Solomon R. Guggenheim Museum; Hilla Rebay was forced out as director; the marvelous collection of non-objective paintings was stored away in the basement, and the dream that Rebay and Guggenheim had worked so hard to realize began to fade. The new administration of the museum changed its original policy and abandoned its purpose. It became just another museum of modern art instead of the monument to non-objective art Mr. Guggenheim had intended.

I cannot explain why this happened, though I do have disturbing suspicions. But my recollection of what led up to that amazing night in June of 1939, and the three people who had the wisdom, guts, and foresight to make it possible, are a missing part of history.

They were the Baroness Hilla Rebay, Solomon Guggenheim, and Rudolf Bauer. I myself happened to be one participant in this amazing story, subsequently injured by the callous shift in museum policy.

Before the Second World War Hilla Rebay was Baroness Hilla Rebay von

Ehrenwiesen. After the war, when she had become an American citizen, she was simply known as Miss Hilla Rebay. She was the one and the only one who could have brought this all to pass. The debt we owe Rebay, and by "we" I mean the art world in general, the painters, writers, sculptors, poets, the struggling, obscure, unrecognized artists across the country, has never been recognized. Rebay was the champion of this small but dynamic avant garde. In the museum these artists had a home of recognition, a chance to show their work, and a great deal of financial assistance through the generosity of Mr. Solomon Guggenheim. Further, through the Baroness's work and that of Mr. Guggenheim, they had an ideal of esthetic based on the museum's masterpieces, including dozens of works by Kandinsky. The collection in itself gave the movement recognition and standing that had an immeasurable influence on artists, dealers, critics, collectors, and the public, and increased the cultural prestige of the United States in general.

The second person was Solomon Guggenheim. Under Rebay's influence he had come to love the new art and to share her frustration that, though it had been around in some parts of the world for almost forty years, it was still the stepchild of "the art world." No museum, critic, or dealer was interested in promoting it. Indifference reigned. It was Rebay who pointed out that an institution devoted exclusively to non-objective art would bring it to the attention of the public. He agreed to help provide the funds to create such a museum.

Guggenheim often said he could only help financially. The credit for the rest of the venture went to Hilla Rebay. She had a vision of a foundation or museum devoted exclusively to Non-objective painting. The problem was finding non-objective paintings important enough to warrant a foundation, let alone the opening of even a small museum. No such supply was available. The best Kandinskys were in museums in Germany.

But there was another artist. Rebay knew of an amazing collection of paintings by Rudolf Bauer, who lived in Berlin. He was, in her opinion, the equal of Kandinsky and in some ways even his superior. But Bauer was holding all his paintings together to start his own non-objective museum in Berlin.

As described in Chapter VI Bauer actually founded his exclusive museum, Das Geistreich, in 1929, and maintained it well into the late-1930s.

Rebay had urged Bauer to come to America several times, even back in the 1920s. But he would not. Berlin was his home. He was adamant.

When Hitler came to power there were all kinds of paintings in Germany, many of them growing out of Kandinsky's work, and German expressionism was prevalent. Hitler told the German people that they were all soldiers in his plan to put the world under German rule. Of course, just before that there had been the big revolution in Russia. The Czar had been kicked out. Russia had a Communist government, and was getting back on her feet after the revolution. The capitalist world was on the side of Hitler at first. They thought he could stamp out the Communist threat and remain always on the side of capitalism.

When Hitler became the Führer, Bauer's hope for his museum's existence faded. Rebay persuaded Mr. Guggenheim to buy the Bauer collection and bring it safely to America. Bauer sold Guggenheim the collection with the understanding that Guggenheim would build a museum in New York to house it, and set up a foundation to support and encourage the growth and influence of non-objective painting. Bauer remained in Berlin for the time being until it became clear that all forms of advanced art, in short, all freedom of creative expression, was forbidden by the Nazis. All so-called "degenerate" art was to be removed from German museums. All of Kandinsky's paintings were to be thrown out as well!

Acting at Rebay's suggestion Mr. Guggenheim urged Bauer to buy every Kandinsky and every non-objective work that came on the market. And so Bauer bought many of the finest Kandinskys ever painted. They came to New York and are now a part of the Guggenheim collection.

First Exhibition of the
Solomon R. Guggenheim Collection, 1936

Some time later Bauer was put into a concentration camp for illegal currency speculation. Through the influence of her family, Rebay was able to arrange for Bauer's release. [Chapter V adds the names of Solomon Guggenheim and F.T. Marinetti (the founder of Futurism) who also aided in Bauer's release from the concentration camp.] Yet he was not ready to leave Germany. In the meantime, a considerable part of his collection and many Kandinskys had come to Mr. Guggenheim. Under Rebay's direction a small exhibition of these works was held in Charleston, South Carolina. When this show was installed Mr. Guggenheim was so impressed with it he had no doubts that a museum should be opened in New York.

The exhibition of The Solomon R. Guggenheim Collection of Non-Objective Paintings held at the Gibbs Memorial Art Gallery in Charleston, South Carolina, March 3 to April 12, 1936, was the first showing of the collection. Hilla Rebay compiled the exhibition as well as writing the catalogue. Included were 62 works by Bauer, 5 by Albert Gleizes, 27 by Kandinsky, 1 by Klee, 2 by Léger, 5 by Moholy-Nagy, 4 by Rebay, and 2 by Edward Wadsworth. Bauer came to America for the show and then traveled to Chicago for an exhibition of his work at the Arts Club, and returned to Europe. A second exhibition at the Gibbs Memorial Art Gallery in 1938 had 95 paintings by Bauer.

When Bauer finally came to America [August 1939], despite a serious language barrier, we became good friends. While in the concentration camp, he told me, he had managed to collect pieces of toilet paper on which he drew up original studies for many of the masterpieces that later became a part of the Guggenheim collection.

Guggenheim came to my studio several times, usually selecting several paintings for his next exhibition. During these visits he also talked at length of his devotion to non-objective art and the joy and satisfaction he felt in being able to present such an important collection to the art world.

What an intoxicating experience it was to go to this museum at no charge and come alive to the wonders of these masterpieces. I felt this myself, as did thousands of visitors. At first a small reactionary group loudly denounced the new art. But as the months went by the objections grew smaller and smaller and within a year had disappeared.

Another view of the Museum of Non-objective Painting is offered by Peggy Guggenheim in her autobiography, Out of This Century: *"After returning to America [July 1941] we went to see my uncle's museum. It really was a job. There were about 100 paintings by Bauer in enormous silver frames which overshadowed the 20 Kandinskys. There was one marvelous Léger of 1919, Juan Gris, a lot of Domelas, a John Ferren, a Calder, a Delaunay and a few other less interesting painters, whose names I don't remember. The museum was a beautiful little building completely wasted in this atrocious manner. Max [Ernst] called it the Bauer House." (Ernst also referred to the Museum of Modern Art as Barr House to reflect the influence of Alfred Barr.)*

Interior of Museum of Non-objective Painting. Hostess usually sat at desk in rear.

Chapter II

I first met Hilla Rebay and Solomon Guggenheim in 1938. I was already an artist, of course, though I didn't make my sole living that way; and I had just come back from England.

Plans for a Target-Guided Missile

The story that follows may indeed be too fantastic to believe, but its credibility is supported by official letters, documentation, and drawings describing the Target-Guided Missile proposal in the Appendix.

In the fall of 1937 I had gone to London on an important mission. I must explain what I was doing there. On the day Guernica was destroyed by bombs, I invented a guided missile. I was on a train, going to New York from Long Island where I lived, when I read the news in the paper. As an artist, my first reaction was to express my horror by making a painting of protest, but something within me called for a greater effort than merely expressing myself that way. The world got the protest of anguish and horror in Picasso's *Guernica*, which is thought of as a masterpiece by great masses of people. I do not agree and think the most that can be granted is that it is a badly organized work exposing Picasso's insatiable ego.

Scarlett was not alone in dismissing Guernica. *Anthony Blount, renowned art historian, curator to the Queen of England, and director of the Courtauld Institute of Art also denounced* Guernica *early in his career but later retracted that opinion (perhaps after he was exposed as a Soviet spy).*

At any rate, my reaction to the unbelievable and cowardly act of bombing that city started another train of thought in me. This would be a new kind of war, worse than any before, with mass killings of helpless civilians, the old, the young, the sick. It was a horrifying idea. I thought, "There must be a way to stop the planes from bombing open cities. In fact, to stop the bombing altogether." From some mysterious source the answer came to me.

By the time I got to New York I had thought out the plan to make a missile guided by a target. So, instead of going wherever I was supposed to go, I bought a pencil and pad and went into a restaurant and sat there drawing up the plans for this device as I saw it. About 4 P.M. I got home and woke up my wife from her nap and said, "Here, get up on the kitchen table. Take this rolling pin and move it all around and I will follow and try to hit it from the floor with this spoon." She said, "What's the matter with you? Have you lost your mind?"

"Well, I don't know, but no matter. You go on and no matter how you twist and turn up there, I'm going to hit that rolling pin with the spoon," and that was the basis for the invention.

She said, "For God's sake, tell me what's going on." So I told her.

"Another of your brainstorms? What are you going to do with it?"

"I don't know. Something."

So I telephoned my friend, Bo Dayvan, in Hollywood. I had worked with him for four years and knew I could trust him. "I've gone a bit crazy." As I laid out the idea his excitement grew. He approved of my plan to call the British Embassy in Washington and said he would come East to help me.

When I called the Embassy, they made no bones about letting me speak to the British Military Attaché. I told him straight off that I was a Canadian living in the United States and I had an idea that I thought could stop airplane attacks on cities. "I have this mad idea and I want to show it to you and anybody else who might be interested.

"Why me?"

"Because — there's going to be a war before long. We both know that. I think England will get a dose of what Guernica got." He asked if it was possible for me to come to Washington.

A week later Bo and I were facing an English officer of a very military cut. I told him what I had, and I hadn't spoken three minutes before he shouted, "My God. My God. That's the answer. The answer to the whole thing. Where did you get the idea? Is it your own?" I assured him it was. "Will you go with it to London? and when? We have got to act fast. Would you repeat what you have just told me. I'll take it down in longhand to avoid the problem of someone overhearing. It will go to London tomorrow morning in the diplomatic dispatch. You will go to London? We'll pay all expenses, of course."

Three weeks later Bo and I were in London. You really cannot beat the charm of the English. Their courtesy, manners, and particular finish. It must be the schools. I have never met a gruff or a poorly mannered one. But they're certainly not fools for all of that.

Our first step was to meet with a Board of Inquiry. The colonel who was our London contact ushered us into his office and we chatted a minute or two.

"Beastly weather, what? Have a cigarette?"

After a few minutes the phone rang. "We'll go along now. The Board of Inquiry is expecting you."

We went down a long hall and came to a door with an envelope, brown with age, tacked on it. It said something like Headquarters of the Royal Airforce Protection Squad of London, a great long title. We knocked and a voice said, "Come in."

It was a good-sized room. Four men in uniform sat at typewriters on one side, four more on the other side, all typing away. In front of us was a long table at which sat some thirteen officers in mufti. One could tell by the cut of their mustaches and their general appearance they were military men, despite the civilian clothes. They introduced themselves very cordially, "You're Mr. Scarlett, yes, well ..." all of them very civil and quite calm.

Suddenly our host jumped up and hit the table in front of me. "Where did you get this idea?" he shouted. Then I saw these were rough guys. They could be very pleasant but they wanted something and meant business. He yelled at me again, "Where did you get that idea?"

"What? Why, I, I thought of it."

Then they started from all sides. "Were you ever here? Were you ever there? We know you were in Switzerland. Are you sure you never heard of this idea any place?" Well, they gave me a real third degree, and my friend too, sitting right there beside me.

After five or six minutes of this, I jumped up. "That ends it. I'm through. What is this third degree? I came over here to give you something and this is how I'm treated. I'm leaving." I was really mad.

"Now wait, Mr. Scarlett, please sit down. I'm sorry but we had to do that. We have to find out all we can about this and we just thought we might surprise you; that you might blurt out something to give us a key. Since we heard of you, our British Intelligence has been checking into everything on the continent trying to find out if there is anything like this in existence. We can't find anything. Please sit down. I apologize for all of us. The international situation is desperate. You know that."

"Yes, I know that."

Then he said, "Do you know anything of the Defense of the Realm Act?"

"Yes, I know of it, how it came into being and so on."

"Could you put all your ideas into drawings and turn them over to the Patent Office? We won't touch them, we won't even look at them until they have gone through the Patent Office. This is for your protection, of course. Take all the time necessary to make the drawings and think out how it should be done."

"Look, beyond giving you the basics, I'm not making any claim to be an engineer or capable of working out the details. It may take teams of engineers to finally bring this thing into being."

"I would expect that," he said. "I'm sure you're anxious to be getting on with it, we've taken enough of your time for now."

As we walked out he put his hand on my shoulder, "Now, just be natural while you're here. Go to the theater. If you have friends in town, visit them. Don't pay any attention to all our precautions. You can rest assured you will be covered all the time. You won't be aware of us, but we will be there all the same. Scotland Yard is very much alive."

If I had known all that before, I probably wouldn't have gone. How I managed not to get my throat cut for my trouble I'll never know. The Germans had planned all along to knock London out altogether. Once they had London out of the way they thought they could easily take over the British Isles. That was Hitler's plan. So these people in London were protecting me. They were going to make sure I didn't get snatched.

Bo and I set to work, Bo taking notes for me while I made plans and drawings for various possible versions of my invention. Once done we took them to the Patent Office. That was in December 1937.

The military people had told me the plans would be sent to them within twenty-four hours of their filing. So I was not surprised when I received a call from one of the colonels at the Board of Inquiry. He asked us to go to Waterloo Station the next morning in order to take the 10:20 train to Woolwich. "I'll be standing under the big clock at the station, wearing a black hat and a carnation in my left buttonhole. Just walk past me. We must keep this as secret as possible. You are to take the third coach up and get in number twenty-four. I'll meet you there."

He did, looking very conspiratorial. Glancing around the compartment, he whispered, "Sh, don't mention anything of what we are about. Just talk about the weather or the shows if you must talk, or the cricket match. Remember, ears are everywhere." After about twenty minutes we got to Woolwich where we got out, and there was a large field maybe forty acres broad. I never saw anything like it. In the middle of the field was a big stone Georgian building.We walked over there from the station. Once inside we found ourselves in a long beautiful room with a fireplace at either end. We were surrounded by a group of very charming young officers, all in civilian clothing, all very agreeable. Well, in no time I was at one end of the room and Bo was at the other end. They were damned smart, those buggers, obviously checking what I would say against what Bo would say. After all, I was a nobody. No one knew me. We were in the very heart of the British Empire being treated like lords. Why? They were very concerned and desperate for an answer.

Oddly, the whole time I was in London I saw only one small mention of Hitler in the news. There was a real news blackout, but those military groups were well aware of the terrible threat. They expected war any day.

At Woolwich, one of my group said, "I say, Reggie, bring us a drink." In a few minutes Reggie came back with tall glasses of gin and Rose's lime juice. Well, with one of those in me my tongue was wagging all right, and that was just what they wanted, to get me tipsy and talking. I think it was then they began to believe I was telling the truth. Bo got the same treatment.

We were called back a number of times in the next month or two and the cloak and dagger routine was always followed. At a final meeting a colonel said, "Don't you think you have given us just about all you have?" "Yes," I agreed, "you have pumped me dry." He then said they would like to have a settlement and asked me to send them a statement of expenses. He also asked if I had any contacts in the United States government that I might use. I realized he was thinking of funding. At that point the British war office was involved with building Spitfires, the planes they hoped to use to turn back the Germans.

I often think,"Who the Hell was I?" This whole experience revealed one thing to me. Here I was, an utter stranger who had popped up out of nowhere. Why did they listen to me? The truth of the matter is, they were God damned frightened of what was going to happen and would have listened to anyone with any ideas. They knew the war was coming and that it was going to be a bad one. And what if France fell? England would have a hell of a time.

Meeting Hilla Rebay

Upon my return to New York in 1938, my wife told me that I had a tentative appointment with Baroness Rebay. "Who is she?" I asked. I had never heard of her. "No, but you will. She is the Director of the Solomon R. Guggenheim Foundation which is devoted to the promotion of Non-objective painting." In answer to a call put out for Non-objective artists, my wife had taken a portfolio of my drawings and paintings to the Baroness, who had responded immediately by saying, "Here is a genius!" The Baroness also invited me to see her to make arrangements with the Foundation for a scholarship to carry on my work.

What an extraordinary person she turned out to be, a dedicated human being if ever there was one. She was strong, energetic, and knowledgeable. Her questions were short and to the point.

"How long have you painted this way?"

"Oh, ten or fifteen years."

"Has this work been shown?"

"Not this work, no. It was never accepted for exhibition."

"Where did you study?"

"Through the usual channels."

"But you didn't study this at any art school?"

"No, I worked this out for myself."

"Do you know the work of Kandinsky?"

"I've seen a few black and white prints."

"Would you like to see some more?" She brought out three or four Kandinskys.

The experience was overwhelming for me, for I was seeing them in full size and color. The wonder of them. The freshness, the beauty. This took the blinders off my eyes and I saw in them the extent of his creativity. These paintings intimately exposed the human soul. They talked to me. They had a sort of cosmic order that made me feel at peace and at home for perhaps the first time in my life. The effect was hypnotizing.

The Baroness interrupted my thoughts asking, "Do you like them?"

"Like them? I'm stunned."

She threw her arms around me, "Yes, yes. I see you know. You have it. This is now your life and you must follow it."

The practical side of this was quickly arranged, and she said as we parted, "Work hard at this wonderful gift God has given you. Soon you must come back again and I'll show you the work of a man you have never heard of, Rudolf Bauer. If you are so overpowered by these lovely Kandinskys, when you see Bauer's work you will be amazed beyond your wildest dreams." How right she was.

From that time on I was tied up with Mr. Guggenheim and Miss Rebay and Non-objective painting. We had no written contracts, but our agreement was that I would continue to paint and would be required to let them have first choice of everything I painted. I was placed on scholarship and they made life very comfortable for me. Mr Guggenheim was a real gentleman and the Baroness a remarkable woman with a bad temper, who could change from a lady into a fishwife in thirty seconds, but nevertheless quite a person.

Chapter III

Childhood and Youth: Guelph and New York

I was born in 1889 in a little town in Ontario called Guelph, fifty miles northwest of Toronto. It had maybe twelve thousand people at that time. Now it has about one hundred and ten thousand. Guelph was an English royal family, and was the only town or community of any kind in the whole British Empire that was allowed to use the name. This was a warrant that old Queen Victoria granted to someone by the name of Clark, who may have been a bastard child of her own husband. It was not a town that attracted immigrants. The residents tried to keep it exclusive, copying the traditional English country structure with a central community of village or town surrounded by estates. It didn't work for long in Ontario. They would bring in their servants and build beautiful homes and cut the forests down and then the servants would vanish because all they had to do was get in a canoe or walk through the woods with a pack on their back some twenty miles away, squat on the land there and they then owned it. So it didn't take more than ten or fifteen years before the idea of exclusiveness disintegrated. But the culture they had brought with them was still there. It had influenced their churches, their libraries, and their homes; there was no other place like it in Ontario.

The whole atmosphere in the town, particularly the section I lived in, was creative and artistic. My grandmother had shown me what to do with paints when I was five years old. The school system was very good and by the time you were twelve you had learned something. This covered the arts as well and I was well-trained in the basics: form, perspective, color, and so on. So with that and my grandmother, I was fairly apt by seven or eight.

There was an all-Ontario children's competition. One day our class got a drawing assignment. We were given three squares and told to render them three-dimensionally, interpret them as blocks, and show their vanishing points. Since it was Christmas time, we also had to include a drawing of a sleigh with kids and toys hanging off it. I was about seven when I won first prize in that competition.

Some years later I sent some pictures to the Toronto Exhibition, an annual affair in Ontario. It still goes on, draws maybe four million visitors in two weeks, covers about twenty-five acres and includes all the products of Canada. Two of my pictures were hung, which got into the Guelph newspaper.

Then an extraordinary thing happened. I was brought up in the Episcopal Church. A Roman Catholic nun had seen the paper. She lived in a convent in Guelph that was also a school for girls, and she offered to give me free painting lessons. So for several years I went to the convent every week. I could hear the girls over the wall, but they disappeared the moment I arrived. Sister Antoinette was a very good artist and had been trained at the Roman Catholic Academy in Rome.

I knew what I wanted to do with my life. I wanted to paint. The only person not in sympathy with my becoming an artist was my father. He was born with a silver spoon in his mouth which by the time he was twelve years old had turned to lead, so there was a bitterness about him. He didn't think the best way to live life was as an artist. He was in the furniture business.

When I was fourteen I told him I was all grown up and didn't want to go to school any more. I was tall and skinny and looked grown. My father said, "There'll be no point in giving you any advice, so I'm going to take the matter in my own hands." He was a quiet man, but a very determined one. He came to me one day and said, "I think I've settled your future. I've apprenticed you for four years to your uncle in the jewelry business."

"Why? I want to paint."

"Yes, I know you do. That's just why you're going into the jewelry business."

Thus I never starved or suffered as an artist. My life was not affluent, but it was comfortable.

My uncle had a beautiful store in Guelph. But to suddenly live my life in the jewelry business, which I didn't like, was very unpleasant. I wanted to paint.

So, after having reached about eighteen working in my uncle's place, I decided to go to Toronto for a vacation. I met my friend Rupert Broadfoot in Toronto. He stayed with one family and I stayed with another. This must have been about 1906. There were no small hotels or motels back then, you either stayed in the big hotel in town or with friends.

One day during this visit to Toronto we saw a sign in a window: Canadian Pacific Excursion to New York Ten Dollars.

Between us we had about a hundred dollars. We figured we could go. We'd have eighty dollars when we got there, so everything would be fine for a couple of weeks, and then we could get jobs if necessary. I could work in the jewelry business and he could work in a pharmacy making up prescriptions. So we decided to run away to New York.

We left for New York the next morning at ten o'clock. They were building Grand Central Station in New York at the time. We arrived at night and walked through what seemed miles and miles of boarded-up passageways.

When we finally came out we didn't know where we were. We looked around and saw lights and went off in that direction. We had heard of Broadway, of course. We came to 42nd Street and 7th Avenue, and realized we were hungry. We saw a saloon, and as there weren't any where we came from, we decided to go in and see what was what. About half-way through our beers a fight broke out between students from two of the colleges in town. They were throwing bottles around and breaking mirrors and smashing up the place; we got ourselves out of there fast.

This time we got to Broadway and walked down it until we finally came to Madison Square Park. From there we saw a great long avenue of lights. "Oh, that must be the Great White Way." It was actually lower Fifth Avenue with all the lights. We had no idea of what the Great White Way was, though we had heard of it. Madison Square Park was an open park; there were gardens and fountains, all quite beautiful.

Pretty soon two women came along and sat down on a bench. They were wearing big turban hats, which they took off and used as cushions to sit on. They were talking in a heavy Irish brogue, passing a bottle of whiskey back and forth, and discussing Joe or Bill or somebody.

We heard a splashing sound and saw a fountain a ways off with people around it, women with their skirts held up above their knees, and men with their trousers rolled up, all splashing around in the water washing their feet and laughing. It was all very strange and very exciting. There were big Irish cops with big bellies and the funny hats they used to wear.

We walked on and after a while I saw a light glowing out of a window up ahead that looked very odd. When we got there it turned out to be a wax corpse in a funeral parlour. Advertising funerals. We hurried on past.

We walked all night, past Union Square, on down and down, and pretty soon we saw a sign that said Wall Street. Well, we had heard of that, we had read about that: the money center of the world. Maybe we could pick up a shilling or something on the street. Luckily we walked down the middle of the street, I don't know why, maybe because the sidewalks were dark and it was light in the middle. We had gone maybe a block, when all hell broke loose.

There was a great big clatter of night sticks hitting the ground and suddenly there were cops everywhere. Two of them had their guns drawn and one said, "You two just stand still there, we'll do the talking. What are you boys doing down here?"

"We're just walking down Wall Street. We've heard of Wall Street and we wanted to see it."

"Where'd you come from?"

"We came down from Toronto."

"Where's Toronto?"

"In Canada."

"Well, what are you doing? walking around seeing the town? All right, don't get in any more trouble. You're in enough trouble already."

We hadn't done anything at all except walk down the street and here there were ten cops around us with guns. The first one said, "Put your shooters away, boys. They're just kids." No one goes down to Wall Street at night. So they thought we were up to no good. "O'Flannery, take these boys up to . . say, where do you want to go?"

"We don't know."

"Do you want to go to the Battery? You can sit in the park there, but don't come back down here again. You're lucky you're not full of holes now.

By then it was very late. We walked on down to Battery Park and saw that this was the end of things. The moonlight was shining on the water there at the end of the island.

I said, "That must be the Statue of Liberty over there." Every now and again the flames would come shooting out of the torch. It was a gas light then.

We sat there awhile until daylight was coming up and we had spent the whole night walking around seeing these queer things, and we were pretty tired ourselves. After a while a cop approached and asked "What are you boys doing now?"

"Well, we'd like to get settled in somewhere."

"How about the YMCA? There's a nice one up on 23rd Street. Take the streetcar and get off at 23rd and walk over about a block. There will be a YMCA where you can stay."

We got a nice double room. Next day I walked over to Fifth Avenue and asked someone how to get to the Metropolitan Museum. It was grand. I walked all around and saw all these great things, and when I came out there was a symphony orchestra playing in a bandstand outside. Right on the sidewalk. How can you beat that? Spend an afternoon in a wonderful museum and come out and spend a couple of hours listening at a bandstand.

I thought I could always write home for money and Rupert could do the same. But we didn't know how tough our parents could be. We never got any money from home at all but my father told me to go to a certain address where I would be presented with a ticket home — bu no money.

So I was cut off and had to find a job, which I did with no trouble. When I finally went home from my little vacation, it was four years later, with a wife and child.

I moved back and forth between New York and Guelph a number of times. In 1913 in Guelph a group of us put on an original musical. The year before we had done a play. You have to understand we were in Ontario and the winters were fierce. We had no television, no motion pictures, no automobiles, we had nothing. There were always several dramatic groups in the town. One might be doing minstrels, another plays, another simple operas. I was in three or four performances before I was eleven. We had ten thousand people and about three million churches. Well, maybe not that many, but more than plenty. All these people went to church, and on Sunday the town just closed up. The pharmacy would open for one hour in the afternoon so you could fill a prescription if you were dying, but you couldn't buy a thing. We did all these other things to keep entertained.

Raised in that Canadian town I was chock full of Gilbert and Sullivan, so much so I had begun to hate them. When my friend, Douglas Crowe, came to see me one day and said, "What are we going to do for a show this year?" I said, "Why don't we write our own?," Douglas asked, "What would it be about? We have to have a plot." That day I was painting a big cut-glass bowl of nasturtiums. I went on painting while we talked and then said, "Let's see. What's going on in the world of great consequence?"

We were British citizens. The suffragettes were raising hell over in London, rioting, smashing windows, chaining themselves to the fence outside Parliament so the police had to cut the fence apart to take the chains off. "How about a light opera using the suffragettes as subject? We'll have a boat that goes to England like the *HMS Pinafore* — we'll call it *The Lemonade Spankhurst* and Bruce will do the music." Bruce Metcalfe, one of our friends, was a musician and composer and had graduated as an artillery officer from the Kingston School of Gunnery, a very snooty place where rich boys went to become soldiers. He was usually our lead actor, very dashing. We all knew how to sing and I had a good tenor voice back then. In New York I was even offered a job once with a touring company.

As we talked I put this song together for the ship's First Officers:

> We both went to college to gain lots of knowledge,
> Learned History, Latin, and Greek,
> But then on real jobs we both are such slobs
> We never have worked, so to speak.
> When we left the last school we made a strict rule
> That we will observe to the letter,

> To live at our ease and do just as we please
> And as loafers you'll find none better.
>
> How did he do?
> How did he do?
> How did he make a hit with this crew?

Douglas interrupted, "What crew?"

I said, "That'll be your chorus on the ship going to England. All girls."

> It's simply because we can handle the bluff
> And we have a way with the La De Da stuff
> Stuff, stuff, stuff. . . .

The show was a big success. I directed it and also wrote the lyrics for the twenty-one songs. We called it *The Gay Pierrots*.

I was still in Guelph when the First World War broke out. I wanted to go and fight for the Old Queen, but they wouldn't take me because of my eyeglasses. They said I wasn't worth killing when I volunteered, so I missed that war and went on painting and doing these various things. And time passed.

A "FIRST NIGHTER" FOR GUELPHITES

EVERYTHING POSITIVELY NEW

The Gay Pierrots

Programme

THE GUELPH OPERA SOCIETY PRESENTS

The Gay Pierrots

A MUSICAL COMEDY IN THREE ACTS

Book and Lyrics by Ralph W. Scarlett.
Music by C. Bruce Metcalfe.
Staged under the direction of Mr. Scarlett.
Mr. Metcalfe, Musical Director.

GRIFFIN'S OPERA HOUSE

FEBRUARY 16th, 17th, 18th, 1914

Paul Klee, Park near L(ucerne), Klee Foundation, Bern, Switzerland.

Chapter IV

While non-objective painting was always my first love, I never set out to make my living exclusively from painting. I always managed very well and met a lot of fascinating people in the process. I was always painting, but got involved in other art activities as well. In Guelph my friend Bruce Metcalfe, a composer, and I put on musicals; I've designed stage sets, at one time even for the Pasadena Playhouse; I've worked for commercial and industrial design outfits; I've made many pieces of jewelry.

Trip to Switzerland and Meeting Paul Klee

Two early events in my career turned me toward non-objectivity. The first happened in Switzerland.

I had worked for P.W. Ellis, a big wholesale jewelry business in Toronto, and through the Ellis boys got to know a man named Simpson, the head agent for the Omega watch company, where I later worked. Simpson told me he was a born promoter and that I should keep my eyes open.

One day a young Swiss came along with a small box full of beautiful watch movements. I called Simpson who came right over. We were amazed to find a wide range of from seven to twenty-three jewel works. A single firm usually did not make a range like that. It was agreed that I would go to Switzerland, track down the company, and see what could be done about importing their product.

In Switzerland I was told that the movements had originally been made for a chain of stores owned by a wealthy Russian who wanted to offer them to all classes of people, from peasants to noblemen. They could be put into cheap cases or expensive ones. We immediately set up a company to handle the watches with Simpson as head.

While I was in Switzerland making these arrangements, Christmas came along and I was invited by Moser, a watch manufacturer, to a dinner party at a grand estate. After dinner I noticed a guest with pen and paper scratching and scribbling. "What's that fellow scribbling over there?" I asked my host. He repeated the question to the man. Then they spoke in French for a few minutes and the man passed the paper to me. "Tell him to scribble some now," my host translated. I scribbled a little but didn't seem to get anywhere. On looking closer, I realized that his scribblings had a definite design, while mine were utterly meaningless. I asked who the man was and was told he was Paul Klee.

When I got back to my hotel room that evening I dug up every scrap of paper I could find and scribbled until four in the morning. That was the moment I left the world of realism completely. It changed my life. I had found something I wasn't familiar with, something in the form of art that had nothing to do with the realistic world we live in.

Years in Ohio and Recognition as a Non-objective Painter

The second event happened while I was living in Toledo, Ohio in the mid-1920s. Toledo had a very fine art center, a good museum, and a very wealthy population really interested in art. There were also various art groups around, one of which I joined. I think it was called the Art Klan Group. I would send my paintings in to the shows. Sometimes they were hung, sometimes I won a prize, sometimes not, but I was part of a group. I also sent paintings to the Toledo Art Museum for their juried shows.

One day I went to a store for some supplies. I bought a canvas or two, and there on the counter were about a dozen boxes of French pastels. I had never seen such colors. There were no such colors in nature. I bought a box. I had been working on an idea of how an atheist would paint a Madonna. One night I noticed my box of pastels, with all the marvelous colors. I took a piece of charcoal paper, put it on a board and set it on my easel. I began daubing colors and a line here and there and I thought, "By God they don't mean anything, just spots and daubs of color, but they are beautiful."

First thing next morning I ran downstairs to look at this thing. It was beautiful. All accidental, not planned in any way. All from a desire to see how colors look. When I sent in my painting to the next show, I sent this one along too. Both were accepted.

At the time I was working in a beautiful jewelry store that catered to a lot of millionaires in Toledo. One day the owner said, "I didn't know you painted."

"Most businessmen don't like art mixed up with business, so I never told you,"

"Isn't this your painting?" he asked. He held up the newspaper and there in the center of the *Toledo Blade* was this thing I had done. (See appendix for review in *Toledo Blade*, April 3, 1926.) This was nearly twenty years before the non-objective movement got established in the United States.

Then a man from the museum called me and asked me to come to see him. When I got there he was sitting behind his desk and as soon as he saw me he started grumbling.

"What right do you have to send in a thing like that to this museum?"

"I didn't know there were any restrictions. I thought it was quite a nice piece."

"Yes," he said. "It won first prize, and we don't have art like that in this museum. What am I going to tell my people who want to leave Gainsboroughs and so on to this museum?

When the show opened the following Sunday afternoon they had to have three cops to keep the people moving through the place.

When I saw people were interested in that kind of thing I did some more. And they sold. So then I had a choice. Should I go on with what what I was doing? Slowly I made up my mind. This was much more fun and much more of a challenge to create things than to copy things.

Move to California in Mid-1920s and Working in the Movie Industry

In Toledo I also got involved in theater. And I met my second wife, Emily, who had two small girls. By this time my first wife Ruth and I had divorced. After Emily and I were married we moved to California and lived in Hollywood for a while. We invested some money in an old market along with a couple of other fellows and remodeled it. All the famous stars of that period came in to see the paintings I had hung on the walls.

One day Ed School, an art director, introduced himself while looking at my work. He was surprised I hadn't heard of him. His first big job was *Birth of a Nation* — he'd been hired by D.W. Griffith.

We became friends. Ed thought my paintings wonderful. He was a good artist himself, producing fine portraits, and had been well trained in painting nudes. As an art director in the motion picture industry, he did just about everything: designing sets, supervising their construction, and seeing that costumes were historically authentic. All the artistic things that could go wrong in a picture were his responsibility. At some point Ed suggested I work in the studio, and I did for about three months. It paid very good money for very stupid work.

I thought it would be an exciting life. I had a big room with desks and drawing boards and such. I would be called in every Monday to get the week's pilots. They would want a picture of a corner of a urinal in a tough part of Paris. Or a picture of a backdoor and path leading up the mountain in Timbuktu, and so forth. They would give me six or eight things they needed. I had to learn to draw these things so that the scenery carpenters would know how to interpret and build them. They would be approved, then there were meetings to check them all out and someone would say, "All right, Lillian Gish will stand here, Dorothy will stand there." I used to think, "Someday I'll get to meet Dorothy Gish." She turned out to be the stupidest little bitch that ever lived.

I also worked for Pathé, a French outfit. Those jobs bored me to death, so I quit. But Ed and I remained friends.

Those Hollywood people were strange. We were living a stone's throw from the Hollywood Bowl in a beautiful section, hills all around with beautiful homes on them. At first I thought it would be wonderful to know such famous people. Six months later I realized they were the silliest bunch you ever met. They didn't have to talk in the old silent pictures, but when talking pictures took over they had to talk and everything changed, because now they had to think too.

Designing Sets at the Pasadena Playhouse and Exhibiting in California

In 1928, my paintings also got me involved in the Pasadena Playhouse, where they put on wonderful shows. Someone who saw my paintings said I must go over and talk to them because they would probably want this new kind of scenery there. (I designed stage sets too.) I went there with a portfolio of my work and when the director saw my designs he said, "These are amazing things." He said they were planning a production of *Man and Superman*. I have always admired Shaw and had seen as many of his plays as I could.

But, I asked, "are you going to give it without the Hell scene?"

"Oh, yes, of course.

"Then it's no show at all. He only wrote the thing to get the Hell scene in. Without it it's nothing. If you'll put the Hell scene in, we'll go to work and do something that's never been done."

"But will the people come?"

"They'll come."

"The only time I've ever seen it done that way was for three days in Stratford as a compliment to George Bernard Shaw. Here we would have to run it two weeks because it takes us two weeks to prepare for the next show. Can you entice a crowd? Can you get attention?"

"Yes."

So we arrived at a price and I went ahead and made my first sketches which I showed him in three or four days. He called them "astounding."

This work had moved into the non-objective world, I realize now, although as far as I was concerned at the time it was still "abstract." So we put it on for two weeks and people came and stayed until half past two in the morning. They'd have a break and go out for something to eat and come right back.

From the review of the play in the Los Angeles, Cal., Record *of November 19, 1929: "the daring and original abstract constructionist settings by Rolph Scarlett have been the occasion of much discussion. . . . the hell scene, because of its tremen-*

dous exactions both on audience and players, is seldom given stage presentation. For these resons the director warned those present that the average audience would probably be happier without it and offered them the opportunity to leave before 12 o'clock [when the hell scene was presented]. Evidently nobody was "average" since so far as I could learn no one took advantage of this offer. Scarlett's settings elucidate the meaning and bridge technical difficulties of costume change and scene shift. It is one of the most significant and stimulating productions ever staged." (Review reprinted in full in Appendix).

On the last day of rehearsal, I was running up and down the stage because the electrician didn't know exactly what to do. I had an orchestra for which I had written music that had everything: motors, a shadow ballet of girls' bodies silhouetted against the cyclorama, lights that flashed to my music, a bassoon and an oboe. Emily had said, "You can't write music." But I told her to write down the notes I hit, then I went and trained the orchestra. I had not seen it sitting in the audience until that day when Emily said, "You'd better see it from the front, because you have no idea of the effect of the thing. People get right on the edge of their seats." It was amazing what happened when the thing got going.

Also, that last night of rehearsal as I was setting up the lights a man came over and asked to photograph the show saying "I've never seen anything like it."

That photographer was Johannes Hagemeyer, the one who taught Edward Weston large-format photography. Hagemeyer was photographing agricultural produce and would go through the fields, picking green peppers or artichokes or whatever and bring them back to the studio to photograph for a newspaper the Department of Agriculture sent to farmers. Weston was working in Hagemeyer's studio and saw the beauty of these things.

The Hagemeyers had recently moved down from Carmel. His wife, Elsa Naess, was a dancer and was teaching dance at the private school Emily's children were attending.

Maybe a month or six weeks after the show finished, I heard from Hagemeyer again and we became great friends. Elsa, a Norwegian, was also a fine concert pianist, and Emily, who played very well, studied with her for some time. Elsa had taken up dance when she came to this country and had studied with Ted Shawn. When Elsa moved to New York she came to work for Hilla at the Non-objective Museum, so our lives were tied together at various points.

Hagemeyer invited me to put on a show of my many sketches and oils at his place. There was a fine review in the *Los Angeles Times* [February 9, 1930] by Arthur Millier, their lead critic, drawing a comparison between Weston's realistic photographs of shells and green peppers and my nonrealism. (See Appendix for review.)

Rolph Scarlett, *Abstraction*, exhibited at Johannes Hagemeyer Studio/Gallery, Pasadena, 1930. (Review by the lead critic of the *Los Angeles Times* in Appendix.)

Decades later when I had my show at Jacques Seligman's Gallery [February 3-24, 1973] in New York, Hagemeyer, on a visit to the city, left a note saying, "I'm very old now but I'm glad to see your show hanging here. I'll never forget the one we did all those years ago in Pasadena."

RETURN TO CANADA AT THE BEGINNING OF THE DEPRESSION AND SETTLING IN NEW YORK IN 1933

I stayed in Hollywood some four and a half years. Then, with the Depression spreading, Emily and I moved back to Guelph for a while with the children. I began to get design work in New York and finally, in 1933, we moved to Long Island.

At first, back in New York, I worked for Design Associates, where we designed anything from thundermugs to baseball bats. Among other things I designed silverware, rugs, and furniture. One of the company's associates got a contract to do sets for Radio City Music Hall. So I designed a lot of the sets where the Rockettes danced. But the contract was in the other man's name, so I didn't get any credit.

Stage set designed by Scarlett for *Man and Superman*, produced at the Pasadena Playhouse, 1929.

Chapter V

Many times during the first four or five years of the Non-objective Museum Rebay would call me late at night to ask me to meet her at Grand Central Station for her arrival the next day. These meetings were always indications of something going wrong with the Foundation or the museum. She would usually be in a highly emotional state over problems of museum policy, or the staff, many of whom she did not trust, or there would be tearful complaints about Mr. Guggenheim and how unfairly he was treating her. Sometimes she lamented poor attendance at the museum or the ignorance of art magazines and newspaper critics. I never understood why she chose to unburden her soul to me, but my sympathy and concern for her were real. I had come to know her dedication and, as I felt the importance of the non-objective movement so completely myself, I agreed with her that anything standing in its way through malice or ignorance should be ruthlessly removed. That made a strong bond between us.

The Non-objective Museum on East 54th Street had been open only a few weeks when one of these meetings was called by Rebay.

This one was about a shipment of pictures by a number of artists the Foundation was assisting, both through scholarships and by buying their work — such assistance was one of the museum's constant activities. The direction of the scholarship fund was under the complete control of the Baroness [Hilla Rebay]. Who else's judgment could she trust in this matter? Who but she could appraise the hundreds of studies sent in by artists hoping to benefit from Mr. Guggenheim's generosity. She was very perceptive, and very little money was thrown away on fakers hoping to jump on the bandwagon. Occasionally, as in the case of Jackson Pollock, her critical sense was led astray by the kindness of her heart, which sometimes stood in the way of her critical sense.

Rebay has been quoted as saying she discovered Jackson Pollock "before anybody else ever heard of him" and gave him a job as a caretaker at the museum "so that he could paint and eat."

The pictures I was helping pack were being sent to the Carpentier Gallery in Paris to show how American painters were responding to the impact of the Foundation and the opening of the Non-objective Museum. There was great excitement among the staff and lots of telephoning back and forth between the museum and the Foundation offices in the Carnegie Hall Building.

One day, I became aware that I was overhearing a protracted conversation between Rebay and her secretary. It seemed to be a three-way conversation, the third party being in Germany. I soon realized that messages were being transmitted in code. This was the middle of July 1939, and the war was not far off. As the afternoon wore on, there was much rushing around and the rumor spread that the Baroness was sailing the next day for Europe.

Late that night the Baroness phoned to ask me to meet her the following morning at Grand Central Station. She was under great stress. She wanted my word that I would go to the museum on Saturday and Sunday afternoons, speak to visitors, organize lecture groups, and generally help the hostesses give intelligent answers to questions. No one else seemed able to explain what non-objective painting was all about, and that applied to the critics of the day as well.

I protested that I did not feel qualified, but she would not accept my refusal. Once I capitulated, she jumped into a taxi and ordered the driver to go to a pier.

Her parting words were, "I'm going to try and get Bauer out of Germany in time."

I was left standing in the station pondering the unpleasant prospect of giving impromptu lectures at the museum.

The Baroness did not have uniformed guards in her museum. She believed that visitors would not damage or molest the paintings, and she was right. So far as I know, no harm ever came to the paintings from visitors. It was so much better to have hostesses who could intelligently answer questions and thus open the way to understanding rather than a large force of guards who knew nothing about the paintings and who created a depressing atmosphere of untouchability and snobbery. The uniformed guards appeared after Mr. Guggenheim died and Rebay was replaced. Whose idea it was, I can't say. It was just another of those incredibly stupid ideas that surfaced as soon as Rebay's influence and direction were gone.

The addition of guards was inevitable because not only had the value of the museum's holdings increased greatly by the 1950s but the museum was now operated as a formal institution rather than as a personal collection under the Baroness's control.

Lecturing at the Museum of Non-objective Painting

On the first day of my assignment, I walked around the museum looking at the Bauers, the Kandinskys, the works by Moholy-Nagy and Rebay, a couple of my own, as well as many more. All were non-objective. The collection was a gem, the effect breathtaking. I felt more inadequate than ever. How could I attempt to explain these masterpieces? True, I had painted this way for over twenty-five years, but it had been intuitive and could not be reduced to words. I expected little positive response to the new art from the average visitor and feared that derogatory remarks would surely come that might lead to unpleasantnesses. I took the elevator to the top floor, telling the hostesses that while the Baroness had insisted I talk to visitors, I had cold feet about the whole thing and I was not to be brought down unless the call was urgent.

It has not been mentioned previously that Hilla Rebay studied painting in Berlin, Munich, and Paris and in the 1920s had a studio in Berlin where she was a popular member of the Bohemian set. Over the years she retained enormous confidence in her talent as a painter.

The telephone rang. A group of art teachers who had made a special trip from Chicago wanted some help with the paintings. The hostess had tried to head them off, but they were insistent. As I stepped off the elevator about twenty men and women were waiting. They asked if I could please help them understand what they were seeing. I hoped they did not know how helpless I felt. As we moved into the main gallery I said, "Well, I've painted this way for years, but it's hard to put into words."

Then, bless my soul, up spoke a bright little angel who obviously saw my embarrassment. "I'm sure you can help us. Let me put you at ease. We've been around this gallery and are thrilled at what we have seen." She seemed to be the leader.

We were standing in front of one of Bauer's great paintings. The silence was painful. Then up spoke the angel again. "The choice of pink that this artist has used in that square is so exciting. I feel sure that all the rest of the canvas swings around it."

"Yes, yes." I jumped in to confirm the observation. "And now that we see that, let's see how he uses the pink again. Yes, there it is way over in the left corner, and see over here on the right is a group of small squares and triangles that carry the same pink." And so the search went on. From squares we traveled to triangles, and as the color changed we found ourselves discovering violets, greens, blues, and so on, while the interest of the group grew and grew. Now I loved them. We spent at least a half hour on that one canvas alone.

Who was most stirred by this experience? I was. Here was the key to putting the experience of non-objectivity into words. Here was a contact with infinity and perfect order. The visitors were responding with joy to the beauty of the visual music that only a painter of this style can offer. It was all there for the asking. All you had to do was look for it with innocence. It was a revelation.

What fun we had then. We went from painting to painting. The original group tripled in size, everyone full of questions and anxious to learn. We were still going strong at six o'clock closing time. After that nobody could keep me from talking at the museum.

Meantime, Rebay's trip had been successful. She had managed to rescue Bauer. This had been accomplished partly through the considerable influence of her family in Germany, but as I understand it, there was also a phone call from Solomon R. Guggenheim to Franklin D. Roosevelt, who may have intervened in some capacity.

RUDOLF BAUER'S ARRIVAL IN AMERICA

Bauer was arrested in 1938 and placed in a concentration camp. The efforts of Roosevelt, Guggenheim, and Rebay could not have been of much help in this situation. But it was more likely Bauer's close friend, F.T. Marinetti, the founder and leader of Futurism in Italy, who had access to Mussolini and persuaded him to intercede with Germany and gained Bauer's release in 1939 and permission for his departure for America.

After a few weeks I had another call from the Baroness inviting me to come into the city from Long Island for lunch to meet Mr. Bauer. For a year or more Rebay had given me the privilege of going whenever I wanted to spend time with the huge collection of Bauers stored temporarily in the old Carnegie Building before the museum opened. The paintings had seemed so aloof at first, so formidable in their ordered perfection and their peaceful beauty. In the beginning I had been overawed. There was a mystery about them that baffled me. Gradually I had begun to know and feel at home with them, even if I could not gather their full significance. Now I was to meet their creator.

I grew nervous as the meeting approached? Was he an egotistical monster? A Prussian bore? A petty, self-assertive sham?

When the moment arrived, there stood a smallish, slim, well-groomed, and somewhat diffident man. He seemed a very genuine person, perhaps a bit retiring, but sure of himself. He was poised and dignified, had a strong handshake and an open smile. His eyes were grey-blue and full of intelligence and wit. I had been foolish. What other sort of person could turn out such paintings?

Even with the language barrier, I believe we felt at home with each other from the first. In the following all too few years my admiration and respect for the man grew.

He used to visit me often when I went to lecture in the museum on Saturday and Sunday afternoons. Often when my lectures were going full swing I would suddenly discover him sitting there smiling as if he was enjoying the efforts I made to make the visitors feel at home with his and

Kandinsky's works. Afterwards when the visitors had dispersed, he would seek me out, grasp my hand, pat me on the back and say, "Gut, gut. Tell me more I did not know." Then he would laugh with glee. I think it was great fun for him to hear me trying to explain his brain children.

Brain children they truly were, because all of Bauer's work is of a very high cerebral quality, joyful but wisely conservative, carried out with authority, yet broadly human. The fact is that about every emotion we are capable of is effectively portrayed in his paintings. This understanding took much time and devotion. Once achieved, the wonder and beauty of these works grew and grew, never did I find them banal or disappointing. Such was the experience of thousands of visitors as well.

Bauer's work was greatly influenced by the music of Bach. He had a violin, and when he felt himself getting a bit rusty would take it down and play, which I understand he did very well. He loved Bach and his work reflected that love. That's not to say he actually translated the music into his visual art, but that just as Bach worked with point and counterpoint and a kind of mathematical precision in music, so Bauer used these themes with paint and canvas.

I found a great similarity between music and non-objective art. The easiest way for me to talk about non-objective art with people who know little or nothing about the subject is to immediately get them off the idea of painting and onto the idea of music. I did that as soon as I could when I lectured by saying that I was going to teach them to listen with their eyes. I took the general position that the paintings were complicated, yet simple. And if a person liked good music he usually liked the paintings. Then I would begin to show them how a painting was organized — very much like music. As a matter of fact, many of the artists used musical terms in naming and discussing their paintings. Three-and four-part compositions were often called symphonies, for example.

There were early signs of trouble between Bauer and Rebay. He came into the museum one Sunday while he was still staying at Green Farms, where Rebay had converted a barn into a beautiful studio especially for him. It must have cost about $70,000. One end was all glass; there was a huge reception room and even quarters for his valet — a palace of a place. After my lecture we went for a drink. I said I was surprised to see him. "I thought you would be out at Green Farms with Rebay."

He said, "Nicht gut. Nicht gut." He explained in part German, part English that he was angry because he had been promised that coming to the United States he would be some kind of king in the art world, flown here and there in a fine airplane and, "What do I get? A broken bicycle." He was really sore because he saw that he was going to play second fiddle to Rebay. Bauer was not going to play second fiddle to anybody without a fight, and certainly not to Rebay. He had made her, and he wasn't going to let her dominate him. Not after having been her teacher and her lover for so many years.

One would assume that Rebay's popularity and reputation as a young artist in Berlin was greatly enhanced by her relationship with Bauer who was then one of Germany's leading artists.

He was supposed to teach at the museum as part of the educational program but had refused. Finally, to please Rebay, or maybe just shut her up, he agreed to try it. Rebay sent out word that he was coming to lecture, inviting particularly those who wanted to bring in work to show him. About a dozen of the nastiest little devils imaginable showed up with a bunch of old coffee cans with bits of wire and paper stuck to them and put this mess down on the floor. Bauer took one look, turned on his heel, put on his hat, and walked out. He never came back to teach again, and he left Green Farms.

I do think Bauer was never happy or at home in America. To the best of my knowledge, he never painted anything here, I have no answer as to why, not even a guess, and he never spoke of it, but he must have felt storm clouds gathering.

Scarlett may have told this story prior to 1970 when at an exhibition of Bauer's work at a New York gallery he was greatly surprised to discover that there were works included he had never seen that Bauer had indeed painted in this country.

He never communicated any hint of this to me. I visited him many times in his home in Deal, New Jersey (where he later moved), a huge place facing the ocean, where he had a chauffeur, housekeeper, gardener, butler, and generally lived like a lord. He had several elegant automobiles plus one great big purple Duzenburg. All bought for him by Mr. Guggenheim, who wanted to keep him happy.

It has been written elsewhere that the automobiles were Bauer's, brought over from Europe.

I would arrive in the morning, bringing a portfolio of studies for future paintings. This was at his request, and there are no words to express the patience and thoughtfulness of his response. He took his time with each piece, looking carefully at each and commenting in German which the delightful young woman who was his housekeeper would translate. "Tell him to do that . . . move that square over there and make it black, and it will all come together." And it would. He never suggested or even hinted at anything that might alter the spirit of the study, but with uncanny sureness pointed out some detail. Maybe only a shift in the position or size of an element, or a change in color or value of the color. The deftness of his analysis and acuteness of his eye were wizardly. Later, when I had finished the large painting from the study, how splendid it was, based on his suggestions.

Rudolph Bauer's villa in Deal, New Jersey.

Chapter VI

The World of Non-Objective Art

Thinking about Bauer and his work I never cease to be amazed. If one man can turn out hundreds and hundreds of such beautiful paintings in one lifetime, the future must be incomprehensible. Great numbers of people creating non-objective art could produce wonderful things never seen before, combinations of colors, rhythms, shapes, as broad as the world and all created visually out of our imagination and developed, just as music has and continues to develop in new forms.

I was brought up in a period when artists looked only to nature for art instruction. That was the entire philosophy of art in the Western creative world. So artists painted a woman's hair and eyebrows and the leaves on the trees, and the more accurately they painted them the better. That was art.

At first I painted landscapes and imitated reality just like everybody else, but slowly I began to get away from it. It would have been very helpful to have heard the term non-objective because that *explains* it. No objects. But the term wasn't yet known. I looked at a thing and then I drew it, though it wasn't very long until the landscape was shoved aside and I was just daubing things here and there in a very haphazard way.

Everything I see in print now about that early period is all wrong. If you asked me what was happening in the non-objective movement before the Non-objective Museum opened, I'd say, "Nothing." That doesn't mean nothing was going on in the world. Nothing was going on in this country. Kandinsky was working in that style from 1904, but the world heard very little about it until 1912 or later. Yet, some art historian or other will tell you Malevich did it before Kandinsky. Malevitch didn't do a damned thing, he stole it from Kandinsky.

There is little documentation to support this claim; the two artists, Kandinsky (1866-1944) and Malevitch (1878-1935), had little in common stylistically. Kandinsky abandoned representation altogether from 1910 on, using bright multi-colors and a free brushwork to create a completely non-objective style. Malevitch reduced art to the fewest possible elements with just a single shape repeated and fixed firmly to the picture plane as in his first "Black Quadrilateral," 1913. As can be seen from the paintings reproduced here, Bauer appeared to be emulating Kandinsky's style and by 1935 had caught up. Anton Gill in Art Lover: A Biography of Peggy Guggenheim *(HarperCollins, 2002) writes: "Bauer was an obnoxious careerist who imitated Kandinsky's style without manifesting a fraction of his talent."*

THIS PAGE:
Left:
Vassily Kandinsky, *Emphasized Corners*, 1923.

Below:
Rudolph Bauer, *Orange Square*, 1935–1937.

OPPOSITE PAGE:
Top:
Vassily Kandinsky, *Improvisation*, 1912. Solomon R. Guggenheim Foundation.

Below:
Kazimir Malevich, *Suprematism: Non-objective Composition*, 1915, oil on canvas. Museum of Fine Arts, Ekaterinburg.

That's the whole point, confusion. It's all jumbled up and nobody knows where they are.

I've been a non-objective painter for almost seventy years, only at first I didn't call myself that. I called myself an abstract painter. But I've been painting in that style one way or another since 1913. Not continually, because I was drawn to different styles, but the more I worked, the more I turned from the world of realism to the world of non-realism. Finally, with Non-objective art, I saw an endless fountain of imagined things coming out of me without any effort and I loved doing it. When you read Kandinsky you see how long it took him to go from the world of realism to the world of non-realism. It wasn't something you did because you saw a lot of other people doing it. You were working it out alone. I didn't make the jump right away. I would do a thing and think it was completely non-realistic, but then I'd find it was something taken from an object. I didn't understand the break at first.

I was under scholarship with the Foundation for four years, while the museum bought my pictures for the permanent collection. Solomon Guggenheim also bought some as gifts. I lectured at the museum on Saturdays and Sundays.

The Non-objective museum was a new idea, not just in this country, but in the whole world. The movement was nourishing a future generation of artists. I had many private pupils too, and some of their work was exhibited at the museum, but I couldn't let Hilla Rebay know about my pupils. She thought I had enormous talent, but still loved to criticize my work and would chalk in corrections that I later rubbed off. (She never knew the difference.) On anything lyrical, you couldn't fool her, but she wasn't good at geometric style and thought. She was very emotional and fancied herself a spiritualist. She would look at Bauer's or Kandinsky's work and read something spiritualistic into it. Kandinsky did that too. It was a mistake. The main thing is not spiritualism or metaphysical phenomena, it's esthetics: order, form, color, and rhythm.

The public has never known how to look at these paintings. Artists don't have a problem; they can create until doomsday and never get to the end of it. Young people seem to like it instinctively. But older ones seem to fear it. "What is it?" they say. "Why do you paint that way?"

I have a method of teaching non-objective painting that is just about foolproof, like a mathematical formula. I can make anybody a non-objective painter. Some are better than others, of course, but anyone can do it if they will let themselves. I learned all that from Rudolf Bauer. It's all very precise, you see, the geometric style.

When I spoke to groups at the museum I wasted very little time. I first said something like, "We are looking at non-objective paintings. There couldn't be a better choice of words because it tells you these paintings are different from paintings of all other times, nations, and cultures, because they have no objects at all. We have geometric shapes. That's all. They are put on a canvas to please you, to intrigue you, to annoy you, or, I should say, to please, intrigue, or annoy the artist, who hopes they will also elicit a response in you. I'm asking you to simply look at what is in front of you."

Then I would go on to talk about some particular picture, a Bauer perhaps, and point out that this was similar to music. Not a picture of music, but music to the eyes. When you listen to music, you can't take it in all at once, it comes to you in a thread. But with a painting the eyes can take it in completely. It has nothing to tell the viewer except its relations of forms. And if you look at it for ten years it will remain a mystery. That is what makes it great. This is listening with your eyes.

We would go from circles to triangles to squares moving slowly, then quickly, then slowly again. Just like music. For the first time they were looking at a picture and not at the man who painted it and not at a three-dimensional object faked on a two dimensional surface.

I once had a great compliment from a young man who came to the museum with a group of students from Pratt Institute. One of them said, "That Scarlett gives me a pain. He's like a god-damned window dresser at Bergdorf. He knows just where to put that last pair of gloves to make the window sing. It's just too perfect." I took that as a great compliment. That's what I learned from Bauer. That's the whole trick — where that last dot goes. You may have the symphony with all its parts but then comes the final note. Without that it's not complete.

Solomon Guggenheim spent thousands of dollars spreading the non-objective movement. Reproductions of the Bauers shown at the museum were sold to visitors for fifty cents or a dollar. Some for a quarter — like giving away free Bibles.

Bauer's Pre-eminence

Rudolf Bauer was a leading artist in Germany, friend of artists and writers throughout Europe, and even founded his own museum, Das Geistreich, in 1929, dedicated to non-objective painting where he showed the works of Kandinsky, Rebay, and mostly his own. The museum was closed to all art dealers with the exception of Solomon Guggenheim, who on one of his collection trips with the Baroness visited and acquired many paintings. The museum continued until the Nazis declared it degenerate and closed it down. However, he has not fared well in art history; although mentioned in Sheldon Cheney's The Story of Modern Art *(NY: Viking*

Above: Rudolph Bauer's museum, Das Geistreich Bauer, An Der Heerstrasse 78, Berlin.

Left: Entrance to museum.

Below: Rudolph Bauer and Filippo Marinetti (right) meeting in museum.

Top, left to right: Hans Richter, Rudolph Bauer, Filippo Marinetti and unidentified man in Das Geistreich, c. 1931.

Below, left to right: Hans Richter, Fernand Leger and Rudolf Bauer at Bauer's estate.

Solomon R. Guggenheim visiting Rudolph Bauer (holding dog), 1936.

Press, 1941), by 1962, when the first edition of H.W. Janson's History of Art *(NY: Prentice-Hall/Abrams) (the Bible of art history) was issued, his name was omitted as it has been in all subsequent revised editions, as well as in other art history books and encyclopedias. What information about his life and works that does exist is in catalogues from his many exhibitions and in untranslated books published in Germany.*

Rudolf Bauer had forty-three pictures in the Guggenheim collection. [*A later count of Bauer's paintings records 350.*] They came over from Berlin in the late 1930s and literally changed the face of art in the world. Yet they were put away in storage in the basement [of the Guggenheim Museum] where nobody could see them. Not because they're not good art, but because Harry Guggenheim [Solomon's nephew and President of the Foundation] hated Hilla Rebay.

Of all the Bauers I am familiar with, I think the two "symphonies" he finished, one in four movements, one in three, are probably the best. They're all interrelated, just as a symphony by Mozart or Beethoven is, but they are visual instead of auditory. Once I showed Bauer some of my own work I intended to make into symphonies. I never found time to do it and now I suppose I never will. But on that occasion I asked him why he didn't do more symphonies as they were so beautiful and I admired them so.

Speaking in German and broken English he made me understand it took too much work and he hadn't the time left. Later I brought the subject up again over drinks. He smiled wistfully and said, "You do it! You do it!" meaning that I should take some of his paintings and make them up into symphonies. I was very flattered. We were very close, seeming to speak the same language in spite of the English-German problem.

So the years went by, until it struck me just recently, that I could take a half dozen of his paintings that I most admire and work them up into symphonies, in homage to his memory, using his colors and his elements. The only question would be whether to make them into two movements or three or four. His work would be acknowledged as his; and mine would be additional. That is done very often in music. Composers of consequence derive inspirational themes from other composers of the rococo or baroque periods. Mendelssohn certainly did. Other important composers took Paganini's themes and created concertos and symphonies. That enriched our musical heritage. I feel the same about the Bauers. I find so many inspirational things in them that could be expanded.

I don't know if I would be successful, but that would be a real challenge for the last years of my life.

Chapter VII

Rebay's Day in Court

Rebay called me one night in 1944.

"Scarlett, please meet me at Grand Central. I'll come in on the 10:20 train tomorrow morning. Don't disappoint me. It's very important."

Greatly curious, I waited at the appointed hour. Soon I saw her barging up the ramp wrapped in a Russian sable coat, a fur turban askew on her mass of auburn hair, an orange scarf flowing in the breeze, an enormous leather suitcase in one hand and a briefcase in the other. She approached with a firm step and as she got closer I could see by her belligerent expression there was trouble.

Rushing up she called, "Come on." None of the usual cheerful affectionate greetings. She was distraught.

She headed for the huge central foyer, backed me into a corner, and stood menacingly in front of me surrounded by her luggage on the floor. Folding her arms, she turned her irate face to me, and asked "Scarlett. Did you ever hear me call Bauer's woman a whore, a prostitute, a slut, or a street walker?"

I was too taken by surprise to answer. "Well, did you, Scarlett? Did you? Please answer me."

"No, of course not. In fact you have never mentioned Bauer's woman, whoever she is."

"Never mind who she is. But you'd swear you never heard me call her any of those names?"

"No, most certainly I never did."

"Then come along." She headed full steam for the taxi stand. As we got into one, she said to the driver, "Take us to the Non-objective Museum. And rush."

The driver said, "Yes, lady. But what did you say?"

"I said the Non-objective Museum."

"It's on 54th Street, east of Fifth Avenue," I added. When we pulled up in front of the museum, she jumped out. I paid the driver and followed. She had already seated herself at the hostess desk on the main floor. When her assistant appeared, she said, "Quick, John, quick. Get all the secretaries, the hostesses, and the carpenters from the basement. All of them."

The staff promptly assembled in front of Rebay, who said, "Now, listen carefully. Every one of you. Did you ever hear me call Bauer's woman a whore or streetwalker or prostitute, or any nasty name like that? Speak up. Did you?"

All spoke up and said they never had.

"And would you swear to that?"

All said yes. "Very well then. Get your hats and coats. We are going downtown." To her assistant, "Quick, John. Get taxis and get everyone into them. Take them to this address on Wall Street."

Shortly we all found ourselves in a huge, swanky reception area in a suite of very posh offices. After a few minutes we were taken into another office where a man was seated behind a huge desk. Once we were seated he said, "You have all been assembled here so that I can read you a couple of letters."

These letters were written by Hilla Rebay, and in them she told Rudolph Bauer that his actions were stupid and reprehensible, damaging to his name as an artist, to her name as a sponsor, to Mr. Guggenheim as his benefactor, and to the Foundation and the museum where his work was so prominently displayed. She asked how he could be so stupidly ungrateful as to live with that nasty little woman who was only a whore, a streetwalker, a slut, and a prostitute. She urged him to get rid of her before the full details of the affair became public.

The lawyer continued that not receiving an answer to her letter, which had been written in a spirit of loving concern for Bauer and all that was at stake, she had written him again three weeks later saying much the same thing. "Now you must see, all you who know Rebay, the high purpose of these letters and what was at stake if Bauer continued to ignore her excellent advice and warning. Now, I want you all to remember the contents of these letters because Bauer has returned the extraordinary kindness of Miss Rebay by suing her for a quarter of a million dollars. Of course she will not be blackmailed that way and the case will be taken to court. Some of you or all of you will be summoned to that trial as witnesses. I want you to remember what I've read and told you. That is all. Good day."

I had suspected that Bauer had a mistress. I always called before visiting his home. His butler would answer the phone and arrangements would be made. One day I got there and rang the bell. A beautiful little creature let me in. When I saw her I thought, "Aha. There have been some changes made."

She was in her late-twenties or maybe thirty, very well dressed and well spoken and poised. All very proper, and obviously a lady. She spoke German fluently and was apparently well educated. After two or three more trips I decided that they were lovers. They were both alone. He had never been married. I guess she was perfectly content to become Mrs. Bauer in time. This was the little lady that Rebay had written about.

Months later I was summoned to appear at a courtroom where the trial was in progress. Only a few of the original potential witnesses were present. Apparently the trial had been going on for several days and, much to my relief, Bauer was not there. Neither was the young woman. I did not have long to wait before I was called to the stand and asked some routine questions by the defending lawyer. The prosecuting lawyer had nothing to ask so I was excused. I think three more were put on the stand, given the same questions and not cross-examined. At this point the prosecuting attorney told the judge he thought enough character witnesses had been called, and since the questions and answers probably would all be the same, the farce should end. The judge concurred. He asked the defending lawyer if he had any more witnesses. He said, "No." Then he asked the same of the prosecuting attorney. He said he did, and that he would like to call Hilla Rebay back to the stand.

Now back to the witness box came Hilla. I must say I felt sorry for her. She looked worn and deeply worried, and apparently not at all happy at being called back to the stand.

And now followed an amazing scene. I did not hear the question the opposing lawyer asked, but Rebay fired back, "No, I will not answer that question."

Again the lawyer tried, "All I want from you, Miss Rebay, is a yes or no."

"Well, I cannot answer that question in a yes or no. There is much more to it than that and I will answer it my own way or I will not answer it at all." She went on and on about that.

Finally the judge, rapped his gavel. At that she stopped in a minute. The judge said, "Miss Rebay. All you are required to do is to answer the question. Yes or No."

"I know very well that he wants me to answer yes or no, and that I won't do. I will not answer him at all because his questions confuse me and I am not going to answer questions for him or you, or anyone else when I am confused." She started to get out of the chair and the uniformed man reached out to either help her or make her sit down. She shouted, "Get your hands off me, you swine."

The judge rapped again, but this time Rebay did not stop. She ran on for forty minutes telling her own side of the case. No one tried to stop her. The judge folded his arms, the prosecuting attorney stood helplessly by, and

Rebay went on and on until she had finished. Then she said, "That is the story and I have told it and that's all I have to say." She stalked out of the witness box and no one tried to stop her. I thought now she had surely thrown her case away.

The judge asked both lawyers if there were any more witnesses. Both said there were not. Looking at the clock, the judge said it was half an hour to noon and suggested recessing the case until the afternoon.

The prosecuting attorney agreed. But the defending lawyer would have none of that. He said, "I beg your Honor to give me the twenty minutes or less to address the jury. Then the case is closed."

The judge said he could go ahead if he could finish by noon.

The lawyer took out the two letters and said Rebay did write them, and handed them to the foreman of the jury to pass around said, "Now let us for a moment forget the letters and grasp the spirit in which they were written. You have heard Miss Rebay tell her impassioned story of why she wrote them. Now, I ask you to see her point of view. She had worked so long and so hard. She had, through her unshakable belief in the cause and style of the art and through Mr. Guggenheim's help, founded a great enterprise and a museum open to the public. All to inspire the cultural tastes of the country at no profit to herself. At no profit to Mr. Guggenheim. All the good that would come of this great effort would be added to the cultural glory of her adopted country. Now she sees all this work cheapened and degraded by the stupid and immoral behavior of this woman. She warns him. She demeans herself by begging him to realize how unworthy his relationshipwith this woman is. Instead of grateful and humble thanks, she is punished and sued. Ladies and gentlemen, this is an outrageous, dishonorable and wicked act that must stain the records of our courts — no, even further — the records of our country, and it need not happen. So I call on you to show the high principles of fairness, decency, and justice that I know are strong in all of you. I'm sure you will return a verdict of not guilty."

By this time, the ladies were wiping their eyes and the rest of the jury looked very uncomfortable. It was three minutes to noon. The case was adjourned until two o'clock.

I was not there to witness the conclusion, having other commitments. But I do know that at about 3:30 Rebay came dancing exuberantly into the museum singing out, "We won. We won. We won."

So much for that incident. But what was the aftermath? I never saw Bauer again. He would not answer my letters, so that great friendship came sadly and abruptly to an end. Even with the language barrier we had gotten on very well. I felt terrible when the trial interfered with our friendship because I worshipped the man. I still do.

Was the suit one of the reasons that the Guggenheim family after Sol's death so ruthlessly removed Bauer's work and nearly eliminated his name? The most wicked part of the whole business is that the magnificent and unparalleled works are hidden away so that neither the art world nor the public can see them.

In the long run, all regrets and hurt feelings pass away, and what remains are the works of art. These great works of Bauer, of inestimable value, should not be stored away and abandoned. Bauer's work should be brought back to the position and recognition it deserves.

Perhaps Bauer's suit, the publicity and the scandal, was one more reason for the Guggenheim family to want Rebay and everything connected with her buried and forgotten.

The New York Times *obituary of Hilla, September 27, 1967, reported that "Miss Rebay was in and out of courts over the years. After she fell out with Mr. Bauer, she was sued for $100,000 by the artist's secretary for allegedly having written a letter in which she called the secretary a 'streetwalker and a spy.' In 1942, she was arrested by federal agents and officials of the Office of Price Administration after they found materials purported to be Nazi propaganda and 1,400 pounds of coffee and sugar, then rationed commodities, in her home. She was held by the F.B.I. for nearly two months on suspicion that she was friendly to the enemy, but the charges were eventually dropped." It has been said that it was Bauer who spread the rumors that Hilla was a spy. In 1963 she faced a minor charge in Tax Court regarding inflated values on donated paintings on her tax returns.*

Chapter VIII

I owe Rebay a great debt. When she discovered me I was completely unknown as a painter, working to develop a non-objective style. She gave me her help, her faith, and her usually patient criticism while I struggled to produce non-objective paintings of strength and beauty. She was a harsh but just critic. So it is with a certain trepidation that I speak of her. I knew her very well for over ten years, and the longer I knew her, the more my admiration for her grew.

When the first of the Bauer collection began arriving in this country in the late 1930s, Rebay arranged for me to spend as much time as I wanted with it. I studied the canvases carefully with increasing appreciation. I made up my mind to do three or four works in this style, that is, with geometric elements. Of course, mine would be just as good or even better, or so I thought. I had several stretched canvases of about 50 x 50 inches and went to work in my Great Neck [suburb East of New York City] studio. After about a month I realized that this method of painting had me licked. I don't mean the painting technique. I mean the *theory* of the geometric themes. The non-objectives I'd done had been in the lyrical style. I was stumped, but couldn't stop.

The paintings got worse and worse. By September, I was so beaten and frustrated I carried the canvases out into the yard and kicked them to pieces. Then I went in the house, called Rebay and told her, concluding, "So, to hell with the whole non-objective movement."

"Take it easy, Scarlett. That's nothing to get all upset about. I've done that myself and I know just how you feel. Now, I'm going to ask a question."

"Go to it, my Baroness. I'll listen."

"Did you make small color sketches of each painting before you started the canvas?"

"No, I didn't."

"Then you started all wrong. I know how simple it looks, but it's not simple at all, and not easy. Get some more canvases. Make careful small sketches, choose two or three of the most beautiful and make enlargements of these on the canvases. It will come out all right." She explained that Bauer always worked from a small sketch. "That's why his work is so great. And you must do the same. You'll see, it will go very easily. Go to it. Goodbye." She hung up abruptly, as she always did.

I had no trouble after that.

Practically all my work for some years was non-objective geometrical. This is the most difficult method of painting I have undertaken. The problem is to create an organization from a few geometrical elements that is alive in color and form, with challenging and stimulating rhythms, making full use of one's emotional and intuitive creative programing yet keeping it under cerebral control, so that the finished work is a visual experience alive with mysticism, inner order, and intrigue, grown into a new world of art governed by esthetic authority.

This form of painting was badly named "hard-edged geometrics." A silly name. It is a great satisfaction to me that I mastered this style, which I believe is the highest form painting can reach.

A Visit to Green Farms

Rebay often called and asked me to come to her home in Green Farms, and if I had some studies for paintings to bring them along. She seemed to take pleasure in looking over the studies in development and was always full of praise for what I was doing and considered me her great discovery. However, it was one of her pleasures to criticize, pick out weaknesses, and suggest changes. On rare occasions she would hit on something I considered a reasonable change for the better, but for the most part I paid little attention. But I enjoyed her efforts and I also enjoyed her company as she was the soul of charm and brimming with ideas for the Foundation and the running of the 54th Street museum. Altogether I found her a delightful person to spend time with and I always seemed a great and important friend to her.

Added to my respect and admiration was her achievement on her own as an important artist. I have slides and prints of some of the marvelous canvases she painted, which are now part of the Museum's Non-objective Collection. They are inspired, great works and when they are seen again, as they are bound to be, I think the world's response will be tremendous. Rebay was also a watercolorist of the first order: I have seen dozens of her fine works in this medium. They are beautifully structured and stamped with her own personality. She also made paper cutouts and montages that are sheer wonders. In this field as far as I can tell she had no peers. Her work is unique in its boldness and originality. She was a very great artist and was most authoritative in the lyrical style, or as it came to be called later, abstract-expressionist.

Hilla Rebay in her studio at Green Farms.

Rebay's Vision for the Ideal Museum

I recall in particular one visit when, after she got tired of criticising the studies I'd brought, we had an excellent lunch. The talk of art in its non-objective form continued. Then suddenly she said to me, "Scarlett, if you were to design a museum, how would you do it?"

I was completely at a loss. I stammered, "Well, I think you have demonstrated so many good points in the 54th Street museum, I guess I would make it something like that. I think a series of rectangular rooms leading from, maybe, a central carpeted hall, and the walls covered with grey hangings as you have them in the museum now. All the walls retire and the pictures dominate the galleries."

"Well Scarlett, you are like everyone else. Did you never think of a gallery that went round and round and up and up leading to heaven?" As she said this she indicated with gestures the general idea of a ramp leading upward snailwise. "Don't you think that would be a priceless idea for a museum?"

The sketch resulting from that luncheon conversation (reproduced here) confirms the originality of her concept.

I had to admit it would be unique. She envisioned it as a place of light and music and spaciousness with the air of a temple in her usual mystical approach to non-objective art. I was caught up in the spirit of her vision and we had a great time planning shows and what would hang where. Before long she had me walking up that ramp to heaven marveling at her ideas.

I asked if plans had been made, an architect selected.

"Not so fast, Scarlett, not so fast. That will come, I have talked the whole thing over with Sol, and he thinks it's a wonderful idea and says I should push it along. But you must be cautious. I do not want the plan talked about yet. It's a secret between Sol and me.

Later, when I saw the first model of the museum Frank Lloyd Wright designed for her and Guggenheim, my mind flew back to that luncheon and her idea of a ramp that led to heaven. I still wonder if she was not the originator of the idea and had persuaded Wright to carry it out for her. Whichever, in my mind it is the poorest museum for art that was ever built. Oh, yes, a showplace for New York City and a rare experience and novelty as a building, but as a museum I think it is a pathetic joke.

After lunch we went to see the magnificent studio that she had constructed for Bauer when he came over from Germany. It was all ready for him.

She herself was now using the huge studio. The walls were stacked with her partly finished canvases. She showed me several and as always I was

This crude diagram will give you a rough idea of how Mr. G and the Baroness wanted the museum permanently set up.

> god.
>
> Bauer, Rebay, Scarlett, Kandinsky
> etc etc etc
>
> Kandinsky, Bauer, Scarlett, Rebay
> Moholy-nagy, etc etc etc
>
> Scarlett, Bauer, Kandinsky
> Rebay, nabel, moholy-nagy
> etc etc etc
>
> Bauer, Kandinsky, Scarlett
> Rebay etc etc etc
>
> street level
>
> current non-objective exhibits.
>
> Lecture Hall
>
> Sub Basement, storage for the following
> Cezanne, Van Gough, Gauguin Matisse
> Legay, Sourat, Chagal, Klee, Braque etc etc
> and so on and on

These are the artists who were not objective, who could not feel who god was.

note the old masters that were to be hung in the sub-basement. This was to show how low and low-hailed they were; and not to contaminate the glory of the elect who were to shine in the presence of god. (So wished all Mr. G. and the Baroness, and it would all have been done if the old man had lived. Ah Rebay.

Rolph Scarlett's copy of Hilla Rebay's vision of the ideal museum.

shocked and amazed. Six large canvases stretched on six easels were occupying her attention at the moment. She said, "Make yourself at home. I'm going to work."

Picking up a tube of paint and a brush she went from canvas to canvas with a perfect sureness of touch. I examined them up close; there was no sign of either pencil or charcoal. This was pure intuitive work. No hesitancy, no painting over, no rubbing out. She would charge from tube to tube, one color after another, if there was any blending or mixing of colors, she did it directly on the canvas. Each canvas was entirely different and each grew and developed as I watched. With all this concentration, she was carrying on a running conversation with me. I was so amazed I asked, "How do you do it?"

"I don't do it, God does it. I am only the agent."

After that I watched in silence, and the more I watched the more my wonder grew.

Suddenly, at about five minutes to three, she asked me to turn on the radio adding, "Please do not talk to me, I want to listen to these programs and as I do not want to be disturbed I'll say goodbye. Nice of you to come."

Before I could get myself together I heard the program start,. Would anyone believe it? One of the slobbery soap operas so popular at the time. As I was in no hurry to get back to Great Neck, I stayed to observe. The painting, from canvas to canvas, went on just as before, but now the tears rolled down her cheeks unchecked. I tiptoed away. Here was obviously a lonely and heartsick woman.

On my drive back to Great Neck I reflected. She had tried and failed to criticize my work satisfactorily although she really wanted to. This geometrical world was not her cup of tea. She had revealed her idea of a museum that would corkscrew up to heaven. She had worked with the mercurial sureness of a driving genius on six canvases at once. And she spent a wretched time with the sloppy sentimental trash that spewed out of the radio.

An Offer to Become Co-Director of the Museum

Some years later, in 1949, when it was evident that Mr. Guggenheim was very ill and would soon pass on, I was visited by Lord Castle Stewart [husband of Solomon Guggenheim's daughter, Eleanor], the titular head of the Guggenheim Non-Objective Foundation. He came twice. It was in the hot summer. He asked if I would go and work with Rebay, quit my job and work with her as co-director of their museum. I wouldn't, because Rebay and I, as much as we cared for one another, couldn't work together. I loved Rebay in a curious sort of way, but knew I couldn't work with her. So I turned down the offer. Stewart called two or three times to see if I had changed my mind. I have no recollection now of how many months passed before Mr. Guggenheim died. [November 3, 1949]. I suppose they wanted me to be there to help run the museum, or their thoughts may have run a little deeper. They may have had an idea that they could get rid of her, then I could be moved up to that job, and perhaps work more compatibly with them. These are just suppositions. It never dawned on me at that time, but as I think it over now, that may have been it.

I never regretted not accepting the offer because I'd have run into Harry Guggenheim [Foundation Board member and later chairman] and, given his hatred of Bauer and all non-objective work, I wouldn't have lasted a week. There would have been a fight. He knew nothing about art. He put in Sweeney as director to succeed Rebay, and he stacked the five-member Board of Directors with four stooges so they could kick Rebay out. *There were actually twelve members on the Board at that time as there have been ever since.* They claimed that the Non-objective movement had petered out. That was sheer nonsense. It was going stronger than ever. And the story that Rebay resigned was nonsense too. She never did. I am amazed at what one rather small group of wealthy and influential people could do.

In order to make sense of this shift in museum policy one must remember the probable enmity of Solomon's two daughters and his other relatives on the Board to Rebay, as long-time mistress to Mr. Guggenheim, and "her artists."

Chapter IX

Hilla Rebay's Stature as Artist and Visionary

Rebay was the driving force behind the establishment of the Non-objective Museum and the promotion of non-objective art, but she was also an important artist in her own right, having achieved considerable fame in Europe before coming to America in 1927. Most creative artists, particularly those with a strong drive, are veiled with layers of self-interest that preclude any interest or inclination to help other artists. This was not so with the Baroness. She was a very generous person, and knowing how hard and callous the art world can be, did all in her power to help struggling artists. Nor was her encouragement reserved for Non-objective painters exclusively, although that style was her passion. Her concern extended to any artist whom she felt to be sincere in his work. She often bought work from unknown painters and even students, and so offered them tangible financial assistance. The paintings she bought were chosen on merit alone, not for any previous reputation the artist may have enjoyed. In fact, she was not the least impressed by artistic reputation. She used her own judgment exclusively, and was almost always right. It was weird to see her go through a shipment of paintings and almost at first glance choose the ones with merit. I think it was this quality of judgment that first impressed Mr. Guggenheim and compelled him to back her.

Of course the Baroness wasn't some kind of saint. She was certainly a kind, understanding, and compassionate person, but also opinionated, aggressive, and often tyranical. She had a dynamic personality and a fiery temper. She was a fighter.

I always called Rebay by her title, Baroness Rebay, or just Baroness. When she became an American citizen, she wanted to be called "Miss Rebay" because she was very proud to be a citizen. But I could never get used to it. She was a Baroness in every sense of the word. I really tried to comply, and speak of her as Miss Rebay, but somehow it was too much like calling "Here, Kitty, Kitty" to a tiger.

There was also her spiritual and mystical side. She often said of her paintings, "I don't do them, God does them." She really believed it. To her, painting in the geometrical non-objective manner was a kind of sacred trust and a striving for divine order. On one occasion, when I not only deviated from this style but raised my asking price as well, she gave me what-for in a letter full of righteous wrath. [See Appendix, letter dated December 14, 1951.]

I got letters from Rebay all the time, about once a week, maybe two hundred in all. She would be hugging me and telling me how marvelous I was, blah, blah, and then end up saying, "but if you don't do what I tell you and take my advice, you'll make mistakes, and go out of the canvas, you'll do this, you'll do that. . . ."

I always answered, agreeing, "You're right, Baroness. I'll do that, Baroness." I agreed with her, then did what I thought best.

In her letters she often criticized my work and my motives. She was often furious with me. But she cared for me. Even when she was furious enough to have her secretary do the writing.

Some examples of her letters reprinted in the Appendix indicate what a difficult taskmaster she was. There was only one way to make non-objective art — her way.

Rebay also had a keen sense of humor and had the knack of turning a potentially embarrassing situation into a fine joke.

Once she was giving a really outstanding lecture on the main floor of the old museum. Of course she was dressed to kill. Rebay was one of Bergdorf's top-drawer customers. She was all wound up that night, holding forth extravagantly about non-objective art, its spiritual qualities, its God-inspired creative aspects, etc.

Suddenly she took a step forward and tripped over something on the floor. She bent over and peered down. "Well, I never," she said. "My underpants. I wonder if God had anything to do with this." Her audience roared with laughter.

As a rule, she had little use for medical doctors. But she did visit some fancy New York doctor on Madison Avenue. His specialty was leeches. Once a week she went to see this doctor and his little leeches. When any of the museum staff were sick, she always urged them to let her doctor leech them back to health. This resulted in scraps because Rebay was used to having her advice followed. Still, as far as I know, none of them ever visited the leeches.

When I used to visit her I would see the huge old photographs on the living room wall — one of a group of very grand people picnicing on a lawn. When I asked who they were, she said, "That's Kaiser Wilhelm II, the Crown Prince of Germany, my father, my mother, my brother, and my nephew. We were having a picnic in a park near Berlin."

Rebay did have some odd ideas about things. Once we had to cut expenses and let some of the men go who worked as carpenters and handymen. One of them was rich and blind in one eye and came from Detroit. I thought he should be the first to go as he had plenty of money and didn't need our help. He was also a bad influence on the others. Rebay refused saying, "But we can't let him go. He has only one eye. Don't you know, every time you give a one-eyed man ten dollars you get a hundred dollars back?"

Rebay's policies at the museum were so extraordinarily different from the policies of most museums that I do not think they were fully grasped. Sol Guggenheim understood them, approved them, and supplied the money to see them carried out, but he was one of the few who did.

Non-objective painting was still the stepchild of the art world. Aside from the small private museum Rudolf Bauer had established in Berlin the movement had no home, no museum of its own, and received very little attention from any established institution. There were large numbers of artists working this way, but still no museum devoted entirely to non-objective painting.

Mr. Guggenheim had been interested in art even before meeting Rebay and had been collecting for some time. He knew nothing about non-objective art, although in Paris he had bought two small Kandinsky sketches, which he said he did not understand. Rebay had introduced him to the new art and he came to love it and to champion it. When the Non-objective Museum came into being, Rebay saw to it that the main purpose of both the museum and the Foundation was to promote the work of unknown artists working in the Non-objective style.

The first museum was rather small. Actually, more space was needed to house just the famous collection of Kandinskys and Bauers. Still, Rebay did not hesitate to give over space to the work of unknowns that began to arrive at the museum from all over the country. She sought my advice about where to hang the works. The first showing of submitted works was hung on the mezzanine balcony. Within three or four months so much unsolicited work had arrived that Rebay decided to give it even more space. Much of the Bauer and Kandinsky work was put into temporary storage so the first Loan Show could be hung.

Still the work continued to come in. Rebay and Sol were delighted at this confirmation of their belief in the need for a place for non-objective artists to show their work.

Acquiring Piet Mondrian's Paintings on the Day of His Funeral

Once, in 1944, when Rebay learned that [Piet] Mondrian was critically ill and close to dying in a hospital in New York, she went there at once. The nurses were coming and going, and outside the door sat Rebay. She sat there on a chair in the hall all through the night, and as the nurses would come out she would ask how he was. Finally, toward the morning around six, the nurse came out and Rebay asked how he was. The nurse said he had just died. *Harry Holtzman and Fritz Glarner kept a 24-hour vigil at the bedside throughout Mondrian's last days.*

Rebay jumped out of her chair, ran down the stairs, grabbed the first taxi she could find and rushed up to a brownstone on 57th Street. She got in and called me from the apartment.

"Scarlett. You must help me."

She gave me an address and asked me to meet her there. It was a brownstone, I remember. I pressed the bell. Pretty soon I heard her high heels tapping on the hardwood floor and the door opened a crack. She peeped out, saw it was me, and let me in, locking the door behind me. She had the key on a string around her neck and she held it out and twirled the key around her finger, and then dropped it down inside her blouse. "There, the bastard won't get it now."

She wanted to buy this man's collection of Mondrian's paintings. She had offered him $75,000 for the lot and he wanted twice that, and she intended to stay locked up there until he gave in and she got her way. She thought $75,000 was a generous price. I thought it was more than generous. I wouldn't have given $75 for the whole damned lot, which was what I thought of them.

Anyhow, she stayed locked in there until he finally agreed. I had to leave, but she stayed until she got what she wanted. She had that tough German jaw and she would set her face so, and you knew she was going to get her way, coming from royalty as she did.

There is no supportive evidence and no registrar's entry of the acquisition of a large number of Mondrian's paintings on this date. The mystery is how did Hilla get the key to Harry Holtzman's private apartment/studio at 358 East 59th St. (close to where Mondrian had lived at 353 East 56th Street before moving to a new studio at 15 East 59th Street, after his second one-person show at Valentine Dudensky Gallery in 1942). Holzman had been supporting Mondrian since the mid-1930s (and was named his testamentary legatee and executor in Mondrian's will), had sponsored his immigration to America in 1940, and had a large collection of his paintings. At first reading it did not seem likely that he would have been willing to part with them immediately after Mondrian's death. However, in speaking to several people who knew Harry, including Martin S. James, close friend and editor and translator of The New Art—The New Life: The Collected Writings of Piet Mondrian *and co-founder of the publication* Transformations, *and Philip Pavia, sculptor and founder of the Artists' Club who remembered Harry frequently selling off Mondrian's works to friends at the Club in the late '40s until his final sale to Sidney Janis [Gallery] in 1951. Also re-assessing the value of $75,000 in 1944 and knowing that Mondrian's works had sold for $200 at his 1942 gallery exhibition, the* *story becomes more credible. But further muddying this story is Hilla's letter in June 1945 (Mondrian died February 1, 1944) to R. Ney in which she writes she "had collected Mondrians when no one would even give $150 for one of them. I own his finest paintings [she actually owned only one] and Mr. Guggenheim does not like the paintings and does not want them." It is documented that she bought her first Mondrian painting in 1930, and that Guggeneheim refused to add any more to his collection, but in 1949 she purchased three additional works and following Sol's death November 3, 1949, she purchased a fourth painting for the museum. Scarlett's account does present an accurate picture of Hilla as grasping and determined to get what she wanted at her price.*

Chapter X

Frank Lloyd Wright and the Guggenheim Museum

Suddenly, [in 1959] well, not exactly suddenly — there was the Guggenheim Museum — the Guggy. An amazingly original piece of architecture. Startling. Impressive. Odd. A round peg in a square hole, a fish out of water, or perhaps as museums go, a snail out of water, made even more bizarre in its Fifth Avenue setting. Why was it there? How did it happen?

The architectural ideas incorporated in the building were taken by and large from the non-objective paintings themselves, and the design was arrived at by studying the work of Bauer and Kandinsky. Now that the building is no longer used for showing non-objective art, its design seems to make no sense. So the new administration's decision to store the non-objective paintings away was indirectly injurious to Frank Lloyd Wright as well as to the Baroness, Mr. Guggenheim, and the artists themselves.

The history of this remarkable building is tied up with the lives of Hilla Rebay, Sol Guggenheim, and Rudolf Bauer, of course. Their dream of a museum devoted to non-objective art bore fruit first in 1939 as the original Non-objective Museum at 24 East 54th Street; again in 1948, in the second temporary museum, a six-story private mansion on the newly acquired property at 1071 Fifth Avenue, and, with the completed purchase in 1951 of the entire block front on Fifth Avenue between 88th and 89th Streeets, construction started on Frank Lloyd Wright's architectural masterpiece [commissioned in 1943]. [The Museum of Non-objective painting again moved to temporary quarters at 7 East 72 Street when its buiding at 1071 Fifth Avenue was demolished at the start of Wright's construction.] I use the words "architectural masterpiece" because any merit due the structure is based on its uniqueness as a building rather than its appropriateness as a museum.

Sometime around 1943 Rebay told me that she [and Solomon Guggenheim] had engaged Frank Lloyd Wright to design the new Non-objective Museum. We had talked about her idea for a spiralling ramp up to heaven since 1942, so I feel sure the original idea was hers. *(See sketch reproduced in Chapter VIII)*.

The plans Wright first submitted showed a series of round skylights around the upper tier of the museum. Rebay said, "Now, that one is mine, and that one next to it is yours, and the next one is so-and-so's." We were all supposed to have studios at the top of the museum.

I said to myself, "No, Baroness, mine will be over there as far as I can get from you." Not because I didn't like and admire her but simply because she was such a dynamo. If I had her next door, I would never have gotten any work done at all. She would have been barging in every five minutes.

Eventually the plans were settled, and the Baroness watched every step of the way. Do not imagine that Wright was allowed to go off and let his imagination run wild. She checked, checked, and rechecked. The museum was hers, not his, although he was the architect who carried out her ideas. For instance, at one meeting I attended with Mr. Guggenheim, Rebay, and Wright, there was a discussion of how the paintings would be hung. Wright wanted to hang the paintings in recesses built into the wall. Once the picture got in there, it was there forever.

Of course that was a foolish idea. It would have been monotonous after a few years. I don't know why Wright suggested it, unless he wanted the paintings to take second place, incidental things stuck into his beautiful walls.

When the new museum opened I wasn't invited, but I went anyway. I stopped at the desk to get a catalogue and went through it page by page. I saw there were no non-objective paintings; it was all expressionism — German Expressionism, Norwegian Expressionism, and Dadaism. The Dadaists, a group of young German [also French, Swiss, Rumanian, and American] painters [and poets and writers] who broke away from accepted art forms early in this century, used various distortions and did things considered outrageous at the time. They were a rebellious crowd, putting their thumbs to their noses and saying, "da da da da da" to all established academic art. So this museum was full of distorted reality of all kinds, but no non-objective art.

Yet Solomon R. Guggenheim had given a large part of his fortune to promoting non-objective art and spent millions on this museum with the understanding that it was to be devoted to non-objective art.

Now here it was, filled with everything else but. That was Harry F. Guggenheim's doing [Solomon's nephew and President of the Board of Trustees]. Once the old man was dead [November 3, 1949] he ran the whole show. After all, what did it matter to Harry if he were sued? If he lost? If he paid a fine? What if it were a million dollars? He had rooms full of money and rooms full of lawyers. Besides, who would question it? For that matter, who even knew the difference between what Sol wanted and what he got, and who would have been in a position to finance such a fight?

Part of it may have been innocent. I'd like to believe it was. Just ignorance. Just businessmen and lawyers knowing nothing about the difference. But I don't believe that, because I know how the Board felt about Rebay and her work and her connection with Sol.

The original exhibition plan for the museum was simple. All the objective or realistic works regardless of the particular style which they expressed were to be hung in their own galleries in a special section of the museum. It was the wish of Solomon Guggenheim and Hilla Rebay to show the progressive development of painting from Impressionism and Cubism to non-objective painting. As far as Rebay was concerned, there was never to be anything on the ramp but non-objective painting. And if Rebay said it, you can be sure Sol said it too.

In discussing the new policy of the museum after Rebay was removed, the Director once wrote, "Stylist limitations were relaxed. . . ." Indeed they were. These stylist limitations were the basic credo of the program that was the cornerstone of the museum and Foundation, the ideal of Mr. Guggenheim and Rebay. These glorious plans have come to ashes. This building that was supposed to be an actual temple to non-objective art has become a showplace of everything *but* that art, while the very art for which it [the building] was created lies hidden away in storage. Not only are the canvases buried, even the color prints of Bauer's work once available through the museum have disappeared. It is as if the work of Bauer, Rebay, and Sol had never been done.

Mr. Guggenheim had expected Rebay to carry out his wishes after his death. He often said to me, "I find it very gratifying to think that my life will have been worthwhile." In the end the plans for the museum and the Foundation had become the most important thing in his life.

The Museum now identified as a memorial to Solomon R. Guggenheim has been vulgarized beyond his wildest dreams. Guggenheim was a fine modest gentleman. It was never his wish or intention to have a museum become merely a monument to him. Now in the minds of many it stands as a monument to Frank Lloyd Wright, one of the outstanding attractions in New York City and one of the most famous buildings in the world.

New York is for the most part very proud of the building. It attracts attention, and people come from all over the world to see it. Unfortunately, they usually show complete indifference to the quality of the art exhibitions.

Wright is certainly entitled to a great deal of credit for his startling architectural achievement. Whether it was actually his idea or, as I feel sure, Rebay's idea which he developed and produced, Wright's genius was stunning.

I did not like the man, he certainly did not like me. And he absolutely hated New York.

I remember the first time I met Wright. The Baroness had called me late at night as usual. "Scarlett, Scarlett, you have to come to meet me tomorrow. You are going to meet Frank Lloyd Wright."

So I was at the station when her train came in. I met Mr. Wright and his wife and daughter, both of whom were very charming, delightful ladies. After the introductions we hurried off to taxis because Rebay wanted to show Wright some of the work at the Museum on East 54th Street.

When we got there he scurried around and looked at this and that, but didn't comment on anything. Rebay took him to the second floor where six or seven of my canvases were hung. She pointed them out with great pride. "These are the ones I've been telling you about." He looked and kind of sniffed, said nothing, and turned on his heel and walked away. He wandered around on his own and finally found the corner where Rebay had hung the "garbage collection" in what she called "the garret." These were unimportant little paintings that Rebay had bought because she realized the painters were young and inexperienced and, though their works were not yet very good, she wanted to encourage them hoping in time they would improve. She generally sent them a check so they could buy more paint or perhaps bigger canvases. These were always her "starving young artists," the hope of the future.

Wright suddenly called out, "Hilla, Hilla, here's a beautiful one over here."

Very excited, he pointed out a miserable little daub about nine by seven inches, of no merit whatsoever, hanging away up in the corner.

She said, "Frank, you're not serious."

He assured her he was. "That's a masterpiece," he said deliberately, trying to be insulting. He may or may not have liked the paintings, but I do not think he liked painters at all. Maybe it was some kind of professional jealousy.

Then we struck out by taxi for a site Wright had proposed for the new museum. As soon as we were in the taxi, Frank on one side, Rebay on the other, and I in the middle, we started up Fifth Avenue and, quickly, off came Wright's little soap dish hat, which he then held up right in front of his face. We were carrying on a conversation and when he spoke he would speak directly into his hat. This irritated Rebay. "Frank, put your hat down. You're annoying me."

He refused. "That hat stays as long as we're riding in Manhattan. I can not bear to look at this horrible place. It is the ugliest city in the world." So the hat stayed in front of his face.

We went on up, past the Cloisters and the [George Washington] bridge and finally came to Spuyten Duyvil. [The most northern tip of Manhattan separated from the Bronx (Riverdale) by the Spuyten Duyvil Creek which connects the Hudson and Harlem Rivers.] There we got out and walked across a couple of acres of land and found some rocks to sit on. Wright said, "Now this is where we should build the museum.

So we sat there discussing the museum. Wright was working very hard to persuade Rebay to agree to locate the museum there. The essence of his argument was that if the proposed museum was placed at the apex of this promontory it would be a monument to non-objective art, Rebay, and Mr. Guggenheim. Rebay was having none of the baloney and retorted, "Frank you're not serious. You know better than that, Frank. It would be a monument to Frank Lloyd Wright."

After listening to the two of them for a while, I thought it was time I said something. "Well, Baroness, now I'm confused. I always thought that the more people who visited the museum, the happier you and Mr. Guggenheim would be."

"Of course, Scarlett, you know that."

"Then I'm really puzzled. How are they going to get way up here?"

Wright spoke up, "They'll come up in their cars, of course."

I replied that I had spent a lot of time at the museum, and assured him that very few visitors come in their cars. "Many don't even have cars, and if they do, there's the problem of driving and parking in New York City."

"Well then, I suppose they'll take the subway."

"I think I should point out that the nearest subway entrance is two and a half miles from here, over on the west side of the Bronx."

"Oh, that's easily fixed. We will have buses meet the subways and pick the visitors up."

"That does seem like a lot of bother, what with subways arriving so often and at all hours, too."

"People will find their way up here somehow when they see the dramatic effect the museum will have. And all the people who will see it as they go up the river to Albany on the Day Line Ships."

"Mr. Wright, while we have been sitting here I haven't seen a single ship, or a boat of any description, or even a canoe pass up or down the river, and the Day Line to Albany has been a thing of the past for thirty or forty years."

Rebay said, "Well, I've heard enough. This is no place to put the new museum. Let's go back to town."

Wright said nothing, but he gave me a look that would have felled a lesser man.

Frank Lloyd Wright, Hilla Rebay and Solomon R. Guggenheim at the unveiling of the model for the museum, 1945.

Rebay had already asked me to go with them again the next day. "I'll call you in the morning," she said. She never did. Wright saw to that.

From a 1960 museum publication, The Solomon R. Guggenheim Foundation, The Solomon R. Guggenheim Museum, Architect Frank Lloyd Wright *with an introduction by Harry F. Guggenheim:*

> The Solomon R. Guggenheim Museum and the collection it houses are a memorial to my uncle, Solomon R. Guggenheim, industrialist, philanthropist and patron of the arts. Solomon R. Guggenheim established the Solomon R. Guggenheim Foundation on June 29, 1937 for the production and encouragement of art and education in art and the enlightenment of the public, especially in the field of art . . . and placed it under the direction of the Baroness Rebay. James Johnson Sweeney succeeded her in 1952 and retained the directorship until 1960.
>
> In 1939 a gallery was rented at 24 East 54th Street as temporary quarters until a permanent structure could be provided. Four years later Frank Lloyd Wright was commissioned and asked to create a new concept in museum design. . . . After acquisition of the entire blockfront on Fifth Avenue between 88th and 89th Streets was completed in 1951, the Solomon R. Guggenheim Museum began to rise.
>
> Neither the donor nor the designer lived to see it in a finished state.

In this 1960 publication, the twelve-member Board of Trustees listed includes Miss Hilla Rebay, director emeritus, as well as Mrs. Harry F. Guggenehim. By 1968, both have been replaced by male trustees.

Harry Guggenheim also credited Hilla's original design: "to the plans of the museum Miss Rebay gave the first design . . . indicating a building with no entrance to be seen, no staircases, but a slowly descending ramp to show paintings without a break of thought or feeling. . . . She has worked with Mr. Wright on the essentials of the Museum for the last eight years."

Chapter XI

The Flim-Flam Man and Ralph Albert Blakelock

In the fall of 1940, a few months after the opening of the Museum of Non-objective Painting on 54th Street, I noticed a rather distinguished looking man sitting in the audience during my Sunday lecture. After I had finished, and the gathering had drifted away, he introduced himself (I forget his name now), saying he would like to talk with me. We arranged a dinner meeting for the next day.

During dinner he told me he was a public relations man and he thought that it was a good time to promote me and non-objective painting. He admitted he knew little or nothing about art, but from what he had read in the museum catalogues about Kandinsky's and Rebay's theories, he felt sure that the spiritual angle would play up very well and he could put me over. With the museum as jumping-off point, he thought the stage was set for a killing. Asked what he meant by a killing, he said, "Well, there ought to be a few millions in it."

I had reservations based on his attitude: imperviousness to the dignity of the museum, the beauty of the paintings, and the sincerity of the writings in the catalogue. Earnestly trying to sell me some preposterous scheme, as nearly as I could see, he had no awareness that the whole idea was a shameful hoax. So I grew curious.

I asked what his experience had been. First, he said, he was a publicity agent for theatrical people; then for years concentrated his efforts on the opera stars singing at the Chicago Grand Opera Company. He assured me no one there got anywhere unless they split their salary with him, fifty-fifty. Now he was willing and anxious to turn all his ability over to the advancement of non-objective art, pulling me along with the riptide, to use his words, "pushing the spiritual angle."

This hustle was just too good to brush aside, so I said, "I can see publicity angles being used with theatrical and operatic people, but not how you could use them to exploit an unknown painter." He assured me he could and if I would come up to his room he would show me convincing evidence of what could be done with proper exploitation of an unknown artist, providing there was a good gimmick.

In his room he pulled out a large suitcase announcing, "These are scrapbooks of some of my successes." I saw various names printed in white on the covers: Nellie Melba (1861-1931), Luisa Tetrazzinii (1871-1940), Amelita Galli-Curci (1882-1963), Edward Johnson (1878-1959), and many more. I said, "I recognize these stars, but none of them are painters."

"I'm coming to what I really want you to see. Ah, here it is." The next scrapbook he held up bore the name Blakelock. [Robert Albert Blakelock 1847-1919].

"Blakelock!"

"You know him?"

"Everybody knows Blakelock's work. Of course I know him."

"Well, I'll bet you and nobody else would know of him today if it wasn't for me."

"That's hard to believe."

He said he and his partner while on vacation in New York visited his uncle, who had a framing shop in midtown Manhattan. Frames were very elaborate affairs at the time, highly decorative, with much carving and burnished gold, and very costly. The shop was sizeable. "After awhile I left my partner and his uncle chewing the fat and, being a nosy type, browsed around the shop. In a far corner I came on several piles of paintings, covered with dust and cobwebs, neglected as being worthless or forgotten. But again nosiness prompted me to turn one of them over. It was a strange, queer looking thing. I picked up another. I knew nothing about art, but somehow I was fascinated by what I saw. I went back to our host and said, 'these are some queer-looking paintings piled in that corner.'"

"They're junk." he said, "No good, just a lot of bother. I'm always intending to throw them out."

"They're certainly crazy-looking. Where did they come from?"

"Crazy? You bet. They were painted by an old codger now locked up in an asylum. He's up at the Middletown (New York) State Hospital for the Insane, mad as a March hare. Yes, they're just nauseating. I'll toss them out some day."

"Then, an idea struck me. Insane painting — insane artist. Hey, maybe they could be promoted along that line and sold. I asked for more details."

"I don't know very much. His name is . . . I don't remember. What are they signed?"

"We went to look and found the name Blakelock. I asked if this Blakelock had any reputation, and how he had gotten the canvases."

"No, no name, he's a nobody. But his story is typical of a starving artist with a sickly wife and several children. He lived somewhere in New Jersey and was befriended by a man named Hearn who had a department store at the corner of 14th Street and 6th Avenue. From time to time he helped

Blakelock out by buying a painting. He put them in elaborately carved frames and decorated the walls of his store with them. Apparently this junk had a certain appeal for some customers, and Hearn thought Blakelock had no one else to turn to for help. Finally Blakelock cracked up, no longer able to take the deal life was giving him, and was committed to Middletown where he eventually died."

"But how did you get the paintings?"

"The framer explained that when Hearn died and the store went out of business, among the fixtures to be auctioned off were a large number of carved frames. 'On the day of the sale I looked them over, saw they were in fair condition, and could be easily restored. I put in a bid and the whole lot was knocked down to me at a few dollars apiece. In the shop, I took the canvases out of the frames. I've made a handsome profit selling the frames. If the man hadn't been such a sloppy painter — see how thick the paint is — I could have repainted the canvases and sold them too. Anyhow they are useless, and I've been meaning to send them to the dump.'"

George A. Hearn was a serious collector of art. His name often appears on labels at the Metropolitan Museum of Art, to which he was a major donor. In 1905 he gave the museum $100,000 for the purchase of art by living American artists. He also exhibited his collection in his 14th Street store, scattered among the goods for sale. Several of those artworks later went to the Metropolitan. — Christopher Gray, The New York Times, *September 15, 2002.*

"The idea that struck me then was too good to pass up. Insane pictures by an insane artist, with a sob-sister life story. Pictures on their way to oblivion. This was a publicity man's dream."

"My partner and I went over the idea again and again that night. Next day we went to the uncle and got an option on the paintings. Then we layed our plans. A reputation had to be set; the artistic value of the work established."

At this point the man opened the scrapbook and there on the flyleaf was a newspaper photograph that I remembered having seen, maybe thirty years earlier, on the front page of either the *New York World* or the *New York Times*, a Sunday issue.

Standing in front of one of Blakelock's canvases was John McCormack, the Irish tenor, handing over a check to one of the other three men in the photograph. The check was for the $100,000 McCormack was paying for the painting. There was also a long write-up about Blakelock and his life.

My host explained that they chose John McCormack "because he was most often ballyhooed and kept in the public eye. His popular standing and integrity made him ideal. The whole campaign was a great success."

As he turned the pages, the list of great museums and important collectors buying the Blakelocks grew. "After the second year we had to pay five or six artists to paint new Blakelocks. Oh, it was a great success."

I asked if John McCormack continued to enjoy his Blakelock.

"Well, I don't know. That check in the picture was post-dated one year. By the time the year was up we had sold so many at much higher figures that he would not surrender the painting. We were stuck with the $100,000."

"Now, do you see how we could put you over? I feel as sure of that as I did about the Blakelocks thirty years ago."

By this time I was thoroughly disgusted and never got in touch with him again.

How many times I've seen Blakelocks prominently displayed in museums across the country, and in private collections too. I always wonder which are the genuine Blakelocks and which are the fakes. But then, who could tell the difference? The truth is they were a very easy job to imitate and well within the capabilities of a competent craftsman.

One earlier episode has nothing to do with my would-be public relations promoter, but does add to the history of the Blakelocks. It must have been about 1920 that I met a charming lady in White Plains, New York. Once during a visit there she asked her husband to show me his private museum. She had heard I was interested in art. This private gallery, which had been built as a wing to their home, was for the sole purpose of housing the small sketches of Blakelock. How he had acquired them I do not remember, but the walls were covered with his small landscapes painted in oils, four or five by eight or nine inches. There were maybe a couple of hundred. He also had a couple of Blakelock's small sketching palettes with paint still on them, hard and dry. I remember being impressed with the vividness of the paint on the palettes, not at all like his finished canvases, which were glazed with deep browns which made them look very mysterious. Why this "molasses pot" when his sketches were sparkling and brilliant? Was this the mark of a sick mind?

Also in that collection was a small landscape by Blakelock and one by his daughter painted while she was in the Hudson River State Hospital. These two paintings were not at all like the finished Blakelocks that are so well known. Neither were they like the sketches in the collection. They could have been painted by any one of the hundreds of Impressionists who were so popular at the time. Certainly there was nothing of that unique mystic quality that is so peculiarly Blakelock. Blakelock's daughter painted in the same style as her father although she was not as good. She used the same surname. She too went mad in 1915 and was sent to the Hudson River State Hospital, then to the State Hospital in Poughkeepsie.

Ralph Albert Blakelock was a victim of his own individuality, financial hardships, and forgeries and exploitations. He was harassed throughout his life by the need for money to support his growing family. In the 1870s, American art was out of step with his work and without a dealer and few opportunities to exhibit he sold any way he could — friends, second-hand art shops and in lots to auction houses. He had his first breakdown in 1891 and in 1899 was diagnosed as suffering from dementia praecox and moved to a hospital. Almost as soon as he was confined recognition of his work came. As demand grew it appeared forgers were producing imitations of Blakelock's style. His daughter Marion sold her own pictures for whatever she could get until she learned an unscrupulous dealer had substituted her father's signature on them. She stopped painting and soon after broke under the strain and she too was hospitalized.

A Blakelock Fund was established by a prominent New York social figure and the work was exhibited in city galleries. In 1916 Blakelock was brought to see one of the shows where he recognized and remembered many of his paintings and identified others as not having been painted by him. A proliferation of forgers produced pictures that were readily purchased by untrained and unsuspecting buyers. A Third Avenue curiosity shop owner in New York had thirty-three Blakelocks for which he had paid $100 for the lot.

(*From Elliott Daingerfield's* Ralph Albert Blakelock, *published 1914, and* The Enigma of Ralph A. Blakelock, 1847-1919. An Exhibition Organized by David Gebhard and Phyllis Stuurman for the Art Galleries, University of California, Santa Barbara, *published 1969.*)

Chapter XII

Some Thoughts on the Difficulties
Between an Artist's Legacy (Paul Gauguin)
and an Affluent Family

So all these paintings of Bauer's and Rebay's and mine are crated up in the basement of the Guggenheim. But it has happened before when there was trouble between an artist and an affluent family. It happened to Paul Gauguin.

I learned this visiting friends in Florida who were artists. One was married to a man who had a very successful real estate business. One day I visited his office and he introduced me to some people, including Mrs. Gauguin.

Later I asked him if she was any relation of the famous artist and he said that yes, she was his daughter-in-law, wife of his only legitimate son, who had been born after Gauguin abandoned his Danish wife. He also told me the family of Gauguin's wife had set up a school of oceanography in Florida and that he had heard they still hated Paul Gauguin with a vengeance.

Now and then I would run into Mrs. Gauguin, and when I asked her about her father-in-law and if she had any of Gauguin's work, she said that yes, she did, and that she would show me what she had. When I went to her house, there on the living-room wall were some Gauguin watercolors. They were painted on letters he had sent his son.

I couldn't believe it. After dinner she showed me more: there must have been eight or ten scrapbooks full. Gauguin would paint a picture and write a letter on it in French and then fold it up and send it to his son. He had made sketch after sketch illustrating what he wanted to say. They were beautiful. Whether the man thought he was laying by a fortune for his son or just being friendly, I can't say.

I was still in Florida when Mrs. Gauguin was taken ill and hospitalized. She developed peritonitis and was dead in a few days. After her death, I heard those paintings were stored in the basement at the school on the shore. The family who hated Gauguin had got hold of them.

The work must have long since moldered away in that dampness in some cubby hole among the silverfish and salt water mist.

It would appear Scarlett's condemnation of their "having gotten hold of them" is without merit, inasmuch as the letters belonged to the family and Gauguin's rightful heirs. Perhaps it is related to Scarlett's identifying with the relegation of these treasures to a basement in a manner similar to the disposition of his own work. However, in this case, if true it was vengeance of a higher order in view of the pricelessness of this trove of letters and drawings.

It is as impossible to guess why the family would have labeled the widow's husband as the "only legitimate son" as it is difficult to reconcile Scarlett's descriptions of Gauguin's tender and loving letters to his son in the widow's collection with Gauguin's almost brutal neglect of his children and their mothers. The widow could have been married to any one of Gauguin's four legitimate sons (all of them born before he abandoned his wife): Emile the first born, 1874; Clovis, 1879; Jean René, 1881; and Pola (Paul Rollan), 1883. Clovis died in 1900 at 21; Emile ended up in America but little is known about him; Polla became an artist and art critic, and Jean René was a sculptor and ceramist. Both Polla and Jean René died in 1961. (There was also a legitimate daughter, Aline, born 1877.)

Gauguin was a successful stockbroker in Paris and had started to paint on weekends, eventually giving up his position and devoting himself completely to his art by 1883. He moved to Copenhagen to live with his wife's family in order to paint fulltime. Within two years he separated from his wife, Mette-Sophie Gad and his children and returned to Paris taking six-year old Clovis with him. He neglected Clovis, pawning him off on neighbors until an aunt placed him in a boarding school where Gauguin rarely visited him. Deciding to leave Paris in 1887 for a brief stay in Panama and Martinique he told Mette to come and pick Clovis up but did not provide any money for her trip. Throughout the years Gauguin contributed little financial support for his legitimate children, leaving Mette with the total responsibility; she supported the children by giving French lessons. Mette was in correspondence with Gauguin until his death, and shortly before she died in 1920 she gave her collection of letters from Gauguin to Polla for possible publication.

On the other hand, Paul Gauguin fathered at least four illegitimate children with island women in the South Seas. His last, a daughter in 1902 whom he probably never knew (he died in 1903), in the Maquesas Islands where he had moved in 1901 from Tahiti. Best known of his offspring is a son, Emile Marae a Tai. The story of Emile's life, as so carefully detailed by David Sweetman in Paul Gauguin: A Life *(Simon & Schuster, 1995), is poignantly tragic. Emile was brought up in Pau'ura and never learned to read or write. In his youth he spent most of his time fishing, sleeping, or drinking. He married in 1920, then divorced his wife to marry another woman by whom he already had six children. He was frequently in prison or wandering drunkenly on the streets of Papeete. His main source of income derived from posing for tourists until a local hotel keeper showed him how a few scribbles on scraps of cardboard could make money by adding his father's signature which he was taught to copy. He continued drinking and painting until, in 1961 the French wife of an American businessman, Madame Josette Girard, installed him in a hut away from the center of town with paint, brushes, and illustrations of Gauguin's work and he started to turn out childlike versions of his father's paintings. Two years later he had a one-man show in London, then Paris, then the United States, where*

Madame turned him over to Marjorie Korler, owner of a gallery in Chicago. Korler installed him in the basement of a building on North Michigan Avenue where he was totally isolated — he spoke no English, only knew a few coarse words in French, and there was no one to communicate with him in Tahitian. He became morose and unable to paint, whereupon Korler sent him back to Tahiti for a recuperative vacation, paying to keep him in a luxury hotel. He soon disappeared and hid at the home of one of his children, leaving his painting career behind. Ten years later when he was seventy-five, a Los Angeles Times *reporter tracked him down and listened to the "story" of his artistic venture, summed up with, "I was no good as a painter." He died January 6, 1980.*

Chapter XIII

Some months before his death Greenberg wrote "I became a pariah while the artists became a legend."

So-Called Art Critics —
Clement Greenberg and Irving Sandler

I have often wondered how art critics get to be art critics. I know of no institution that confers the title on these frequently conceited nincompoops. Beyond their questionable appraisal of their own ability they seem to speak by Divine Right, the stock-in-trade of European monarchs. Of course there are a few men and women who are knowledgeable, experienced, and well-educated, with the good judgment and ability to write with intelligence and sensitivity in the field of art. But these seem to be the exception.

Just because someone writes an article on art and then has the luck to have it published, should he be proclaimed an art critic? And this cultural impostor may be applauded by the most interested parties — the artists, the dealers, the collectors, the museum directors, and of course that mob of loud-mouthed bores who "just love art" and spend their time yapping about things they know nothing about. I have read book after book, and article after article, and find the worst of this pompous babbling appears in the art magazines.

In the past fifteen or twenty years this bunch of clowns has perpetrated a real burlesque on the art community. I am willing to make allowances for growth and also to extend tolerance to a small group of established and responsible men and women who for some reason remain ignorant of some very important facts concerning the broad field of non-objective art.

One must be reminded that Scarlett's reminiscences are from tapes made from 1970 to 1982, and if nothing else, his self-confidence is impresssive.

But what is one to think when a critic with an excellent reputation, in covering the work of an artist of the Abstract Expressionist school, makes it a point to inform his readers that the Abstract Expressionist movement began with Jackson Pollock and makes no mention of Kandinsky, as if Kandinsky's lyrical non-objective canvases had never been painted or exhibited in New York? Or when a book by Irving Sandler, touted by the Book-of-the-Month Club as "an important contribution to art history, crammed with information," and so well documented as to rank as a source book, makes no mention of the opening of the Non-objective

Museum in 1939. Yet all of the fifteen artists featured in the book were grown men and practicing artists in 1939 and more than likely visited that beautiful museum.

Irving Sandler's Triumph of American Painting *referred to the triumph of the "new" abstract expressionists in New York City as the break-through moment when New York deposed Paris as the center of the art world and chǎnged the face of American art. Art dealer Daniel Henry Kahnweiler was the first to note "the center of painting has shifted and New York has become a modern Alexandria, an international metropolis of the arts."*

"The most visible avant-garde group in the late 1930s was American Abstract Artists and for most of them the mystical content that underlay the work of Kandinsky and the other artists hanging in Rebay's museum posed no problem since they were mostly unaware of it. . . . [The] presence of the influential teachers from the Bauhaus such as Moholy-Nagy, Albers, and Gropius lent authority to geometric abstraction." (From Martica's Sawin's Surrealism in Exile *[MIT Press, 1995]).*

It is more likely that the New York artists (estimated to number between 125 and 150 at the time) were aware of the museum since John Graham served as secretary there for a while. An artist and theorist, writer and curator, Graham was a legendary figure in New York's art world. He had an imposing physical presence, was greatly admired, and exerted significant influence and authority among his peers. In 1937, he published System and Dialectics of Art, *which codified advanced art thinking in New York and established him as "the reigning art guru of modern taste."*

There [at the museum] they would certainly have seen a large number of Kandinsky's non-objective works, some in the lyrical non-objective style in which manner he painted in 1908 and for some time thereafter. His style was shown clearly in the first Armory show in 1913. While most of the modern work did not receive broad attention at the time, Kandinsky's work received wide publicity and was well known in art circles from coast to coast and in Europe.

Rudolf Bauer's work was also being shown here and in Paris between 1920 and 1939 (Anonyme Show, November, 1920; Société Anonyme Art Museum, December, 1920; Société Anonyme New York Gallery, 1923; Museum of Modern Art, October, 1933; Charleston, SC, Solomon R. Guggenheim Collection, 1936 and 1939; one-man show, Musée du Jeu de Paume, Paris, 1937; Baltimore Museum of Art, Guggenheim Collection, 1939).

I have set out this list to document Bauer's exhibition history, and to show that both Bauer and Kandinsky were widely exhibited in this country before anyone ever heard of Abstract Expressionism. Hundreds of their lyrical works were shown over this long period of time and it is completely unrealistic to believe that none of the abstract painters had seen and been influenced by the abundance of lyrical non-objective painting in their transition from Realism or objective painting to non-objective painting and thus to what was called Abstract Expressionism. Some of these painters were probably painting in the lyrical manner and the phrase "Abstract Expressionism" was no doubt coined to identify their *new* style

I imagine angry protests, and a clamor for proof. I hope so. That might force the Guggenheim's present administration to bow to public interest and put on a huge show of the hundreds of Kandinskys, Bauers, and other non-objective painters of the 1920s, '30s, and '40s now buried in their basement, (*Kandinsky's work has never been "buried in the basement"; actually the paintings are in a warehouse.*) or as they put it, "placed in storage for safety's sake." Then those interested in the art history and culture of this country decide for themselves whether these were the source of much inspiration and direction for the Abstract-Expressionists.

Clement Greenberg, who coined the phrase "abstract expressionism," knew nothing about abstract art and nothing about expressionism, but he did know something about words. So he put the two words together and came up with a new phrase that was meaningless and confusing.

Actually, the critic Robert Coates is thought to be the first to use the term in 1946 and it was officially recognized in the MoMA exhibition of 1951, "Abstract Painting and Sculpture in America." In 1952, Harold Rosenberg used the term Action Painting and Clement Greenberg described the work as American-type painting, differentiating it into brush painting concerned with gesture, action, and texture and Color-field painting.

I met Clement Greenberg in a roundabout way. Emily and I have been married fifty-two years now, and she and I brought up her two daughters from a previous marriage, Elizabeth and Barbara. When Elizabeth grew up, she married Delmore Schwartz, a poet, who was an editor of *Partisan Review*, where Greenberg got his start writing.

Delmore told me that Greenberg wanted to write about poetry or write book reviews. But the other editors didn't think he knew enough to write about literature, so they told him to try art.

At dinner with Delmore, Greenberg said,"Art critic? What the hell? I don't know anything about art." (That time he told the truth. He still doesn't know anything about art. He may know even less now than he did then.) Delmore told him it was simple, "Go to the galleries. Talk to people. Visit the museums. Ask questions. Talk to artists. New York is full of galleries and museums. You'll learn the jargon, whether you know art or not."

Before long Greenberg was guiding people through museums and going to the artists' studios to criticize their work. So, he knew nothing, still knows nothing, but he learned some tricks. When he faced a picture, he would look at it very seriously for a long, long time. Then he would say slowly, "Ah, um, yes. A master statement."

During that period, the early days, I was painting in the geometric non-objective style and from time to time Delmore Schwartz came to my studio. One day he brought that jackass Greenberg with him. Greenberg looked all around and had little or nothing to say. After they had been there a good while drinking my gin, Delmore said, "I brought you up here to Rolph's studio to show you what he does and see whether you think it's contemporary of the times we live in."

Finally, with great brilliance, Greenberg said, "Anyone who paints today is a fool. In ten years we will have blown ourselves to Hell and the pictures will be no good anyway. Nobody's will." This was a year or two after the bombing of Hiroshima. He thought the only way for artists to respond was to paint pictures with no content or very little content, all in one color, preferably a depressing color.

Finally in walking about the studio, he saw an old rag on the floor. It was about ten inches square and had been white cotton before I wiped my brushes on it. It was all daubed over with black paint. Greenberg picked it up and said, "If you can paint a series of pictures like this I'll make you famous."

I said, "Then you'll never make me famous because that's not a painting, it's just a piece of garbage I threw on the floor."

As it happened, I was at that time doing quite well and didn't need him to make me famous.

Then, as the years passed, I began to see in the *New York Times* and the art magazines pieces by Clement Greenberg, or others saying Greenberg thinks this, Greenberg thinks that. What the Hell? He's a good enough writer. He knows how to handle words. But it's like taking a blacksmith to the symphony orchestra — because he is used to the hammering noise of his anvil he feels capable of criticizing what the orchestra is playing. Greenberg was in the right place at the right time with the right friends. But it was the wrong thing for art. In my opinion, his stupid criticisms probably had much to do with killing what was going on in this country.

On the contrary; Greenberg's writing and influence were contemporaneous with the most productive period of art in America and its premier position in the universal art world.

When Greenberg was at my studio, I asked him if he had visited the Non-objective Museum on East 54th Street, in particular to see the works of Bauer and Kandinsky. As I remember it, he replied, "Most certainly not. I wouldn't bore myself with that experience." This was the mouthpiece of the Abstract Expressionists.

Peggy Guggenheim

Peggy Guggenheim (1898-1979) was the daughter of Solomon's youngest brother, Benjamin Guggenheim, who died in the sinking of the Titanic. She became part of Bohemian life abroad before World War II. During the days just before the fall of France, Peggy made it a point of honor to buy a painting a day from working artists. Although she was not a great connoisseur of art, she had good advisors and was an active collector of art, and friend, patron, and lover of many artists and writers. Peggy became known for showing new art, first at her gallery in London and later in New York, at the lavish Art of This Century gallery, which she opened in 1941 upon her return to America. After its closing in 1949, she moved her collection to a palazzo in Venice, where she remained for the rest of her life. She bequeathed her collection to the Guggenheim Museum, "my uncle's garage, that Frank Lloyd Wright thing on Fifth Avenue" as she referred to it some two months before her death, adding, that the gesture "was rather a joke since I wasn't on very good terms with my uncle."

Peggy [Guggenheim] detested Sol and Rebay and everything they did and was of great influence in the Abstract Expressionist movement. Rebay only accepted pure geometrical non-objective painting for the Solomon Guggenheim Collection. So Peggy liked to collect Rebay's rejects and promote them to annoy both her Uncle Sol and Rebay. Her entourage included James J. Sweeney, Clement Greenberg, and Max Ernst [husband]. And, if I am not mistaken, a good number of the fifteen artists featured in Sandler's book were first shown at Peggy's gallery and their works became part of her "Art of the Century" collection.

Of the fifteen artists included in Sandler's book, only four, Pollock, Motherwell, Rothko, and Baziotes were given one-man shows, and by 1945, deKooning, Gottlieb, and Reinhardt had been included in group exhibitions.

Peggy, who was known as a collector, curator, and critic, often said, "I know nothing about art." Nevertheless, she had considerable influence in the art world.

Hilla treated Peggy with great disdain. The following letter reprinted from Peggy's book, Out of This Century, *was Hilla's response to her asking her Uncle Solomon if he "still wanted to buy a Kandinsky that he had so long desired."*

> Dear Mrs. Guggenheim "jeune"
>
> Your request to sell us a Kandinsky picture was given to me, to answer.
>
> First of all we do not ever buy from any dealer, as long as great, artists offer their work to us themselves & secondly will be your gallery the last one for our foundation to use, if the need to get an historically important picture, should force us to use a sales gallery.

It is extrememly distasteful at this moment, when the name of Guggenheim stands for an important art, to see it used for commerce so as to give the wrong impression, as if this great philanthropic work was intended to be a useful boost to some small shop. Nonobjective art, you soon find out, does not come by the dozen, to make a shop of this art profitable. Commerce with you cannot exist for that reason. You will soon find you are propagating mediocrity; if not that you are interested in non-objective art you can well afford to buy it and start a collection this way you can get into useful contact with artists, and you can leave a fine collection to your country if you know how to choose. If you don't you will soon find yourself in trouble with commerce.

Due to the foresight of an important man since many years collecting and protecting through my work and experience, the name of Guggenheim became known for great art and it is very poor taste indeed to make use of it, of our work and fame, to cheapen it to a profit.

Yours very truly,

H.R.

To be generous we could attribute the viciousness of the letter to Rebay's poor command of English.

Exhibiting in the Whitney Museum, 1951

Why the term Abstract Expressionism prevailed over [Rebay's term of] lyrical non-objectivity, I don't know, except for the Guggenheim family's hatred of Rebay. This was evident to me from an experience at the Whitney Museum. I had gone to see the Whitney Biennial. As always I was disappointed at not finding anything except Realism and Surrealism, one way or another.

But one year, 1951 maybe, the Whitney Museum came to my studio and made a selection of a painting for their exhibition. The painting they selected had a history.

One Saturday morning in my studio on Irving Place, I was feeling bored. I had a pupil there, Maude Kerns. She had come from South Africa and been studying with Hans Hoffman, but became a pupil of mine after visiting the Non-objective Museum. I had been working with great concentration on a geometric non-objective, when on a whim I got out some cans of enamel paint, blue, red, green, black, white, and more. I put a painting I didn't care about on the floor, then punched holes in the cans and dribbled the stuff over the various things on the canvas.

My student asked if I'd lost my mind. I said I was having a helluva good time.

I left the canvas on the floor. When I came back Monday morning the paints had hardened and run together in a most amazing way. I decided not to go in to work that day. My studio was located adjacent to the firm for which I worked; they had three-fourths of the floor and I had one-fourth. I called up and said, I wasn't going to work until the end of the week. I usually worked for them three days a week but made my own schedule. So I spent the next three days working on this new painting.

When the man came from the Whitney Museum, I showed him my latest geometrics. The new "lyrical" one I had dribbled on was on the side. He asked if it was new, and when I said yes, he chose that one for the show.

When the show opened my painting was featured in the newspaper with its own write-up. The critics on the *Times* and other newspapers had chosen it for discussion. So what began as a joke and an accident in a mild way became quite famous.

Non-objective vs Abstract Expressionism

The day of the opening I saw that as usual the exhibition was ninety percent Realism and Surrealism. There was a group of young people, maybe twenty or thirty, all looking at my picture and talking about it. Finally, one girl came over to me and asked if I were Mr. Scarlett. When I said I was, she asked what I called the painting. I said it was a "lyrical non-objective."

She replied, "non-objective is a dirty word. We don't use it here. That is Abstract Expressionism, nothing more, nothing less." She turned on her heel and walked off.

Clearly they had been trained to hate the word "non-objective." What had started with the Guggenheim family had spread to the dealers and the public.

When Rebay came to my studio to see the painting, she liked it but would not buy it for the collection, telling me with considerable annoyance, "You know very well that I will not have it in the permanent collection. I will not buy that sort of work from anyone."

I knew that only too well, but there were times when I wanted a rest from the difficult, exacting work of conceiving, developing, and painting a really fine "geometric non-objective." That was the most difficult of all forms I worked in — also the most rewarding.

Over the years, critics and commentators have played up various angles of artists' lives and habits and the paintings themselves to promote them. Sometimes, as in the case of poor old Blakelock, it was their "mystical" quality. Sometimes it was the old doomsday theory espoused by Clement Greenberg. I remember back in the fifties and early sixties, it was the artists' suffering. "No pain, no fame." It was all very silly and in retrospect it is hard to believe that such issues were actually a part of art.

Well, I still have no answer as to how art critics become art critics. Many of those who are well known and influential are the first to proclaim they "know nothing about art." They seem almost proud of it.

Chapter XIV

Tribute to Baroness Hilla von Rebay:
Guggenheim Museum Exhibition, 1968

In April and May of 1968 the new administration of the Solomon R. Guggenheim Foundation gave a Memorial Exhibition for Hilla Rebay. You might ask why this exhibition was held at all. Hilla had been cruelly neglected, insulted, and degraded after the death of Mr. Guggenheim almost twenty years earlier in 1949.

Those who know the truth about the history of the Foundation and the Guggenheim Museum were sickened by what was so vindictively done to the memory of a great woman. Given my debt to Guggenheim, Rebay, and Bauer, I feel I must set out the facts to do what little I can to redeem her memory, since the Memorial Exhibition projected a false image, as it was no doubt intended to do.

First of all I was shocked to see the mean little space it had been allotted. That in itself was heartbreaking. Then, when I had studied the catalogue and read the contemptible foreword, written by Mr. Thomas Messer, the Director, I found it degrading to Rebay's memory. But there it was in black and white, so full of half-truths and sly, destructive innuendos that I was filled with hopeless frustration.

I am quite sure the ultimate decision about space for the exhibition and the selection of paintings from the permanent collection was made with the approval of the head of the Foundation and members of the Executive Board. The exhibition was ostensibly to honor Rebay, whose vision of a museum dedicated to non-objective art had been shared by Solomon Guggenheim. That was not the intent of this exhibition.

The sly and deliberate title in the catalogue should have been enough to warn me then.

It is difficut to attribute slyness to the forthright title — "The Solomon R. Guggenheim Museum, Acquisitions of the 1930's and 40's A SELECTION OF PAINTINGS, WATERCOLORS AND DRAWINGS IN TRIBUTE TO BARONESS HILLA VON REBAY 1890-1967."

I was shocked to see which paintings had been hung, including one of her least important works in the collection, one that I knew Rebay had considered destroying. When it was hung in the museum on 54th Street she said how unhappy she was with it, adding, "Some day I'll take it home and destroy it." But here it was, the vindictive choice in this, her memorial show.

I was further shocked at the selections from Rudolf Bauer's paintings. Practically all of Bauer's work, some 250 to 350 paintings, are owned by the Foundation, with the exception of those owned by the Louvre and private foundations. A superb collection of Bauers and Kandinskys and the works of other non-objective painters, the original backbone of the Guggenheim's collection, had inspired the creation under Rebay's direction of the Foundation, in the first place. The Guggenheim Museum was built to show this collection.

The five Bauers in the show included *Orange Accent* and four unimportant studies called *Tetraptychen 1, 2, 3, 4*, that were done in 1936. *Orange Accent* is one of Bauer's less important paintings done in 1929 or 1931. It's a fine work, but so simple in conceptual treatment that the esthetic wisdom of it is easily overlooked. It shows the capacity of the man to *whisper* great truths rather than speak in his usual voice of authority. When it hung in the 54th Street museum it was very popular, but it was a trivial and unfair choice to make from all his great works.

The *Tetraptychen* as a choice for this show was almost criminal — they were only studies or sketches for a great work Bauer had planned. They were also a bone of contention between Rebay and Bauer. She had hung them in an inconspicuous place in the 54th Street museum and Bauer wanted them removed. But she liked them, so he humored her and gave in. It must have taken quite a diligent search among the Bauer masterpieces to come up with such an unimportant painting and four paltry sketches. It would have been better to have shown none at all.

Now, one comment only about the petty treatment I received. Through the years Mr. Guggenheim had bought about sixty of my paintings for the permanent collection. I consider them my life's best work and I was proud to have them in this wonderful collection. However, after the death of Mr. Guggenheim, my pictures and those of Bauer and Kandinsky were all put in storage and, during these many years, never shown. *(This is certainly not true of Kandinsky's work which has always been prominently displayed at the museum.)* This caused me great loss of prestige and loss of artistic recognition, as well as financial hardship. The picture of mine chosen to hang in the memorial show was a good enough small monoprint, but not an important work. Again, this contemptuous attitude to my work was a slap in the face to Rebay and Bauer as well, the current administrators being perfectly aware that Mr. Guggenheim never bought any paintings without the approval of Rebay and Bauer.

The reference to Kandinsky's paintings being put into storage is patently incorrect. The museum has mounted a major show of his paintings and considers his work one of its major holdings, devoting nine pages (the most for any artist in the collection) in their publication, Guggenheim Museum Collection A to Z, *published 2001.*

The Memorial Exhibition Catalogue with its so-called tribute to Hilla Rebay, written by Thomas Messer, is deceitful. The opening paragraph sets a tongue-in-cheek attitude for the exhibition.

The first two paragraphs from the catalogue, reprinted below, appear to be even-handed and accurate.

> Acquisitions of the 1930s and 1940s is presented in tribute to the Guggenheim Museum's first Director, the Baroness Hildegarde von Rebay von Ehrenwiesen. The works here exhibited besides many others came to the Solomon R. Guggenheim Collection in the first phase of its institutional existence through her initiative.
>
> As a painter, translator and pamphleteer, the Baroness in her day was known as the stormy petrel of non-objective painting — a mode of abstraction that excluded recognizable subject matter from the vocabulary of the visual arts. Her passionate espousal of Rudolf Bauer, Moholy-Nagy, Scarlett, Nebel, Xceron, Mondrian, Kandinsky and of many others bore out in action her strong convictions and beliefs. The roster of acquisitions however transcends the non-objective limitation and contains works of quality and importance in a variety of styles.

There is no obvious deceitfulness in the catalogue, but perhaps there are subtleties only recognized by Scarlett.

It allows a trickle of praise to Hilla for helping Mr. Guggenheim assemble his collection of non-objective paintings. It does not mention that it was Rebay who cajoled Mr. Guggenheim into accepting the idea of the Foundation in the first place. He often told me how the Foundation was Rebay's idea, and how under her urging and towering influence he became the willy-nilly sponsor and financial backer of Non-objective painting before he was quite aware just what it was all about.

Joan M. Lukach in Hilla Rebay: In Search of the Spirit in Art *describes the diminishing importance of Rebay: "After her death her role in founding the Museum of Non-objective Painting was forgotten and she achieved a secondary role as having been merely an advisor to Solomon," and the Guggenheim Family biographer, Edwin P. Hoyt, Jr., also delineated the collection as "the great art was collected by Solomon and the weaker ones in the collection chosen by Hilla.*

Several times the catalogue refers to the "first phase" of this institution, leading the unwary to believe that there were different, well-planned phases in the short life of the Foundation. There were no "phases." It must be understood that Rebay did not urge Guggenheim to set up a Foundation for just any art. It was a special kind of art. The Foundation was established to open a museum and to give non-objective art a recognized home. Rebay and Guggenheim even went further, dedicating themselves to the task of promoting the geometrical style of non-objective art.

It would appear that Scarlett is not recognizing the range of the paintings acquired by Rebay during her tenure which Messer generously acknowledges: "Matisse, Rousseau, Seurat, . . . the group of gem-like canvasses hold a very special place among Miss Rebay's great acquisitions."

And how is one to react when early in the catalogue one reads, "The Baroness was known as the 'stormy petrel' of non-objectivity." To call Rebay a "stormy petrel" is as ridiculous as calling the Rock of Gibralter an ant hill. She was a roaring lioness when she was fighting for non-objectivity and all it meant to her and to so many of us dedicated to its growth.

The dictionary defines "stormy petrel" as a person who causes or likes trouble or strife. Inasmuch as Rebay was not known to avoid confrontation this does not seem too far off the mark.

The catalogue also implies that during the time Rebay was director of the museum, from 1939 to 1952, she hung many of her own paintings as part of the original collection. This is not true. I lectured there from the second week the museum was open until the latter part of 1944, so I can speak with authority. Many interesting things happened, but I want to make clear that Rebay did not hang her own work in the museum and hog the show as is implied.

The catalogue is so full of contradictions and deceptions that it is hard for me to write about it with the clarity I want for the historical art record.

I should explain why all the figurative canvases shown in the tribute to Rebay were originally bought for the Foundation. I went over this with Rebay and Guggenheim, many times. Figurative painting stood many, many cuts lower in their minds than non-objective painting. In the anticipated museum, it was planned that the figurative paintings would be hung in the basement galleries, while the upper galleries would house the non-objective paintings. Visitors, helped by well-instructed hostesses, would see the virtues and artistic qualities of both kinds of modern painting, and recognize the purer esthetic values of non-objectivity. That was the vision.

Although Scarlett acknowledges Rebay's purchase of paintings other than non-objective, he stubbornly refuses to recognize their importance to the collection. Messer, however, gives generous praise to Rebay's discernment:

> Hilla Rebay's attitude toward the Cubists was ambiguous. . . . she rejected them in their later, figurative phases. However, here again the distinction of the acquired Picassos, Legers, Gris, Gleizes, and that of such Orphists and Futurists as Delaunay and Severini speaks admirably for the clarity of conviction that gathered them under one roof.

Figurative content, resisted by Hilla Rebay in the pioneering phase of abstraction, was acceptable in the mannered portraiture of Modigliani, the fantasies of Chagall, Klee, and Campendonck, and in Marc's and Kandinsky's der Blaue Reiter. The addition of Klee's work to the Guggenheim Collection was among the most important measures taken during Hilla Rebay's administration. . . . Intuitive taste and personal bias came to its happiest conjunction in the Baroness' championship of two separate avant-garde movements that had telling consequences for twentieth-century painting: the painters around the Dutch group of De Stijl and the masters of the Bauhaus. The former, gathered around Mondrian, counted among their ranks Van Doesburg, Vantongerloo, [and] Vordemberge-Gildewart who, thanks to the Baroness, are all represented in the Museum Collection today. Even more rounded is the Bauhaus collection which in a large part was brought together before the creation of the Guggenheim Foundation when Hilla Rebay visited the Dessau center as Solomon R. Guggenheim's artistic arbiter. Moholy-Nagy, who came to the Bauhaus in 1923, attracted the Baroness' interest and as a result is represented by no less than 45 works. Other Bauhaus masters gathered from the same source include Klee, Feininger and, of course, Kandinsky, whose massive representation in the Guggenheim Collection remains without any doubt Miss Rebay's most dramatic contribution. Those remembering the early phase of the Guggenheim's functioning will recall that it was primarily Kandinaky's canvasses which together with Rudolf Bauer's and those of the Baroness herself were in evidence throughout the first Director's administration that lasted from 1937-1952.

There is nothing grudging in Messer's admiration for Rebay's acquisitions and he is discrete in acknowledging that the collection was uneven — as was inevitable when on occasion an artist's entire oeuvre was purchased by Rebay.

True, some small gratitude is due the administration for the memorial show for Rebay, even though it was such a paltry affair. It did at least show the great discernment, wisdom, and sureness of Rebay's knowledge of all types of art. Even in the catalogue this is grudgingly admitted.

However, elsewhere, Mr. Messer ungrudgingly gives Hilla full credit: "Hilla Rebay proposed the original Guggenheim Museum theses . . . . and after Sol's death the museum replaced the non-objective faith with a variety of idioms."

The Baroness put together an incomparable collection of non-objective paintings. Nothing in the world even approaches it. So why was she kicked out when Mr. Guggenheim died? The catalogue says she resigned. I do not believe that; and no one who knew Rebay would believe it. Concurrent with her ousting, all the non-objective paintings of Bauer, Kandinsky, Rebay, Scarlett, Moholy-Nagy, Xceron, and many others were put in storage — Why?. There has never been a satisfactory reason given for this dishonorable act. Mr. James J. Sweeney became director at the time. Many of us in the art world ask if it was his idea or if he was just the hatchet man.

The works of Kandinsky and Moholy-Nagy are shown regularly and listed in the latest Guggenheim Museum Collection catalogue

Rebay was an astute art judge. But in finding or collecting modern *figurative* art, one almost always has the security of established, recognized names. An art authority should obviously be rated on the astuteness he or she brings to the judgment of a new and unknown work. That is the real test. How many have the guts to trust their own appraisal of an unknown artist's work and stand by their decision? Rebay and Sol belonged to that rare group. She knew what was worthwhile in all periods of painting, far beyond the abilities of most critics. She was also a rock in supporting her decisions, which, of course, did not make her a very popular person.

The final two paragraphs of the catalogue: one of which is generous enough to grant the sincerity of the work, are ill-disguised condemnations of Rebay and Guggenheim's finest achievements. It would have been preferable never to have printed this shabby and deceptive tribute at all. Rebay should be honored for her gifts to the Foundation, the city, and the nation. Even today it is not too late to carry out her original inspired ideas: The Foundation is there; the museum is there; the great collections of Bauer and Kandinsky are there. All that is needed is a change in heart and an administration that will carry out the original intentions of Rebay and Guggenheim. Further, conditions today are more advantageous than in 1939. Non-objective art is accepted, the capacity to create this way is there and the great need for leadership could be met. How marvelous if this could come to pass.

The final two paragraphs from the catalogue, which Scarlett finds "shabby and deceptive" are reprinted below:

> It would be too much to expect an even qualitative texture from as passionate a collector as was the Baroness. That acquisitions made in her time include more than their share of masterpieces is demonstrated through the current selection beyond any doubt. Although not unaccompanied by lesser works and by flaws which, in keeping with the Director's temperament also came decisively and in round numbers, it is the highlights which stand out today as the Baroness' legacy emerges firmly buttressed by the great works that adorn the permanent Collection of the Solomon R. Guggenheim Museum.

Acquisitions of the 1930's and 1940's — a selection from a large reservoir of works — cannot, it must be admitted, claim the sanction of the personality it honors. The Museum's first Director would certainly have stressed the non-objective idiom for its own sake more than we have and there can be no doubt that Rudolf Bauer's, her own work, and that of artists here omitted would be given more prominence in a choice reflecting Miss Rebay's own preferences. To accept these for the occasion without modification has of course suggested itself. If such an alternative was abandoned, this was done because it seemed preferable to let a great contribution benefit from hindsight so effortlessly gained so that the result may stand, if not as intended, then certainly as fated.

Meanwhile the catalogue is full of deceptions and half-truths.

I believe the exhibition was a gesture of atonement for the way the Guggenheim had treated Rebay, but they did not feel they had to do a decent job. This could even be overlooked, except that it betrays the attitudes that have demoted the Guggenheim Museum from its former position of unparalleled importance, even acclaimed as leading the world of art, to a museum of little or no importance to the world. It is an almost unbearable desecration of the high ideals of Guggenheim and Rebay for the museum to fall to the tenth-rate position it now holds in the mind of those qualified to judge. (*Scarlett would indeed be surprised by the museum's current enviable position.*)

If one needed further confirmation of the breadth of Rebay's art purchases, René Gimpel in his Diary of an Art Dealer *enters in his diary of July, 1939: "The Baroness de Rebay is coming to have dinner at my house. The taste of this apostle of cubism is for the fantastic; for instance, she bought hundreds of Bauers because of their sexual charm. She has taken one or two poor Picassos only and one or two Braques, so as to exalt her favorite. She is the Catherine II of this school. However, as a moving spirit she's not without a genuine spark." And in a later entry, "The Baroness made some remarkable criticisms of [William Hayter's] paintings. She put her finger on the weakness with an almost cruel precision. She was nearly as clever in her criticism of the engravings. . . . She bought an engraving from him for $15. She cannot brook the least recognizable human form in modern art."*

Chapter XV

RUDOLF BAUER EXHIBITION, NEW YORK, 1970 AND
HOW THE NON-OBJECTIVE MOVEMENT WAS WIPED OUT

Late in November, 1970, I received a phone call from a friend. "There's a large show of Bauers on Madison Avenue at the Leonard Hutton-Hutschnecker Gallery."

This was too fantastic to believe. "That's impossible."

"I'm telling you it's so. In fact, I've just come from there and it's a very impressive show. They even have several paintings from the Guggenheim.

The year before, early spring, 1969, without much fanfare, the most extensive show of works from the permanent collection at the Guggenheim was opened to the public. Naturally, I was very anxious to see it, as I expected a good selection of the work of Bauer, Kandinsky, Rebay, Moholy-Nagy, and some of my own as well.

So, making one of my infrequent trips to the city, I went directly to the Guggenheim reception desk to buy a catalogue before seeing the big show. Imagine my surprise when I was told no catalogues were yet available. The receptionist said the show was up and the catalogues would be out later and one would be sent to me. As I climbed up the tiresome ramp, I became more and more baffled, then upset, and finally outraged to find there were no Bauers, no Rebays, and certainly no Scarletts. Most of the works that had been acquired during the early years of the museum when Rebay had been director from the 1930s through the early 1950s had been omitted from this large show. Aside from some Kandinskys and a few Moholy-Nagys, none of the top notch non-objectives were shown at all.

Why had the bulk of the non-objectives been deleted? The dirty work that had been going on since Mr. Guggenheim's death was still going on. The museum that owned most of Bauer's work was trying to obliterate his reputation as an artist.

So now, some of Bauer's paintings were on loan? Much as I hate to go to New York City, I had to, and a few days after the phone call I was at the Hutton Gallery. Sure enough, there was a really smashing show of Bauer's work. I recognized many of the large canvases as those I had lectured about at the old Guggenheim Museum when it was on East 54th Street.

But there were also many unfamiliar canvases. Where had they come from? Mr. Hutton told me the paintings I was not familiar with belonged to Mrs. Bauer. Apparently, Bauer had married that lovely and charming young lady and before he died had given her all the paintings he had done in this country and many early ones that the Guggenheim Museum did not own. This was a surprise, because with the exception of eight watercolors now owned by the Yale Museum and one owned by the Louvre, all his early works were owned by the Guggenheim. So he had painted in this country after all.

Mr. Hutton said the Guggenheim had loaned him fifteen Bauers from their permanent collection. They had also promised to put on a Bauer show at the Museum, but so far had not done so, and as near as he could see were not going to.

Hutton had printed a splendid catalogue for the show and gave me a copy. He said this was the fifth showing of the Bauer collection, after shows in Cologne, Brussels, London, and Weisbaden and all had been great financial successes. Of course, he hoped his efforts in New York would pay off too. That evening as I was looking over the catalogue I came across a long itinerary of Bauer's work, and there I saw the date of the Cologne show, September 12 to October 15, 1967. And the shows had been going on ever since. Yet in the big show at the Guggenheim Museum, Bauer's work had been conspicuous by its absence.

The European shows revived interest in Bauer and were followed with several exhibitions in the United States in 1989 (Los Angeles) and "Anniversary Tour Remembers Rudolf Bauer" in 1990, Chicago.

Chapter XVI

Homage to Hilla Rebay, Exhibition, Carlson Gallery, University of Bridgeport, 1972

When Sol died he had already made Rebay a very wealthy woman. She had the wonderful two hundred acre estate, Green Farms in Connecticut, another mansion up in the White Mountains, and I don't know what else. He had turned all this over to her with the idea that when she died her estate would be used to establish a center to further the teaching of non-objective painting. I think it was partly because he did not trust his nephew, Harry Guggenheim, to do this. This was a dream enthusiastically shared by Rebay. When she died, I naturally wondered how their plans would be carried out.

Some time after her death I saw an article in the *New York Times* which told at great length how the estate of Baroness Rebay had been turned over to the University of Bridgeport, and that they had mounted an exhibition of Rebay's collection, including several Bauers. I called Harriet Tannin, a friend of mine, and asked if she would drive me from my home near Woodstock, New York, to Bridgeport. With the chance to see more of Bauer's work, Harriet said, "Sure, let's go."

The show was well worth the trip and we were both glad to see the work of Rebay and Bauer. Now things get a bit sticky. The catalogue was small and beautifully illustrated in color, but right inside the cover were two representational prints, one of a rather poor Chagall, the other a Delaunay. This was really an insult to Rebay's memory.

Had Rebay been alive, she would have made sure that any exhibition in homage to her would be purely non-objective. It had been her whole life. I asked the guard who had hung the show and he directed me to the man's office.

He was a pleasant and agreeable man. I asked him about the catalogue. He said it had not been set up under his direction but by a member of the governing body of the Foundation. When I inquired if I could see this person, he told me that he was with a firm of lawyers with offices in Greenwich [Connecticut]. I asked if I could call him from this office. He promptly got him on the line for me and I told the lawyer about my friendship with the Baroness and asked him if I could see him for a few minutes. With some reluctance he agreed to give me fifteen minutes if I could be in Greenwich shortly.

In Greenwich, after waiting a few minutes, Harriet and I were asked to come in. Seated behind a desk was our man, not looking too pleased to have his busy day interrupted. But with cold New England manners he wanted to know why I was interested in Rebay. I told him again of our long friendship and how closely we had worked together for ten or twelve years, and he thawed out some. "What is it you want to know?"

I told him I had read the article in the *Times* and asked if it would be possible to know some of the wishes of the Baroness as set out in her will.

"Yes, of course you can. You said your name is Scarlett?"

"Right."

"We have three or four of your canvases in the bank vault where we have Miss Rebay's property."

"Could I see them?"

"Yes, of course. I'll take it up with the members of the Board who administer her estate. Could you get in touch with me in a couple of weeks? I will take you over to the vault and you may see the will, as it is open to the public."

I thanked him and said I would be glad to take advantage of his offer. Then I said, "You are very decent to do this and I want to congratulate you on the splendid catalogue you produced for the show." I held it up and he looked very pleased. "But there is one little matter, you see. It is well organized and splendidly printed and bound but there are two pictures that are not the non-objective art she promoted."

I looked very innocent. He said he did not know the difference between a non-objective painting and any other kind, and "I don't think any of the others on the Board would know either, because the Board is made up of three lawyers and two businessmen."

"Well, who did oversee the catalogue?"

"When we have to make decisions about things we are not familiar with, we have to turn to the administrative group in the Guggenheim Museum, Mr. Messer and his assistant."

Disposition of Rebay's Estate

It was exactly what I had expected to hear. Then I went on, "You see, I'm tremendously interested. Am I asking too much if I inquire what is to become of her beautiful home Green Farms?"

"As the will states, all the income from her estate is to be devoted to furthering the growth of non-objective art. There are to be a lot of scholarships and the income is to be devoted to the advancement of non-objective art."

"Yes," I said, "I'm sure that would be the Baroness's dearest wish. Is the school already in operation?"

"No, that will take time, but I'm sure it will get started soon." It never did. The estate was never used for that purpose.

Then I asked how James J. Sweeney came to be the director of the Guggenheim Museum. He said that Baroness Rebay had recommended him. I jumped from my chair and said, "Good God. You must be pulling my leg."

A couple of weeks later I wrote to make an appointment to see the will and visit the vault. I did not get an answer, so I let a couple of weeks pass and then telephoned to set up a visit as he had promised. Of course, the girl who answered the phone asked my name and said she was very sorry, he was too busy to talk to me. I tried several times more, but he was always busy. Then it dawned on me that the Guggenheim tricks were going full blast again. So the next time I called I said, "Tell him it's an old friend. I want to surprise him."

He swallowed the bait. Then I told him who I was and asked when I could make an appointment to see Rebay's will. He said that the offer had been withdrawn and I could not see the will. And I never did.

Apparently Scarlett was not aware that the will was open to public scrutiny and he had only to appear at the court and make his request. From Joan M. Lukach's Hilla Rebay: In Search of the Spirit in Art: *"Although Rebay's will stipulated that Fanton Court [and Green Farms] be used as a museum and research center, it proved impossible after her death and the trustees of her Foundation agreed that the Guggenheim Museum should care for the paintings, library, and the more than 10,000 letters and documents she had amassed. The house was eventually sold, but the surrounding acres continue as a bird and wildlife sanctuary as she had intended."*

(See appendix for text from catalogue essay by Bruce Glaser, Director of Exhibition.)

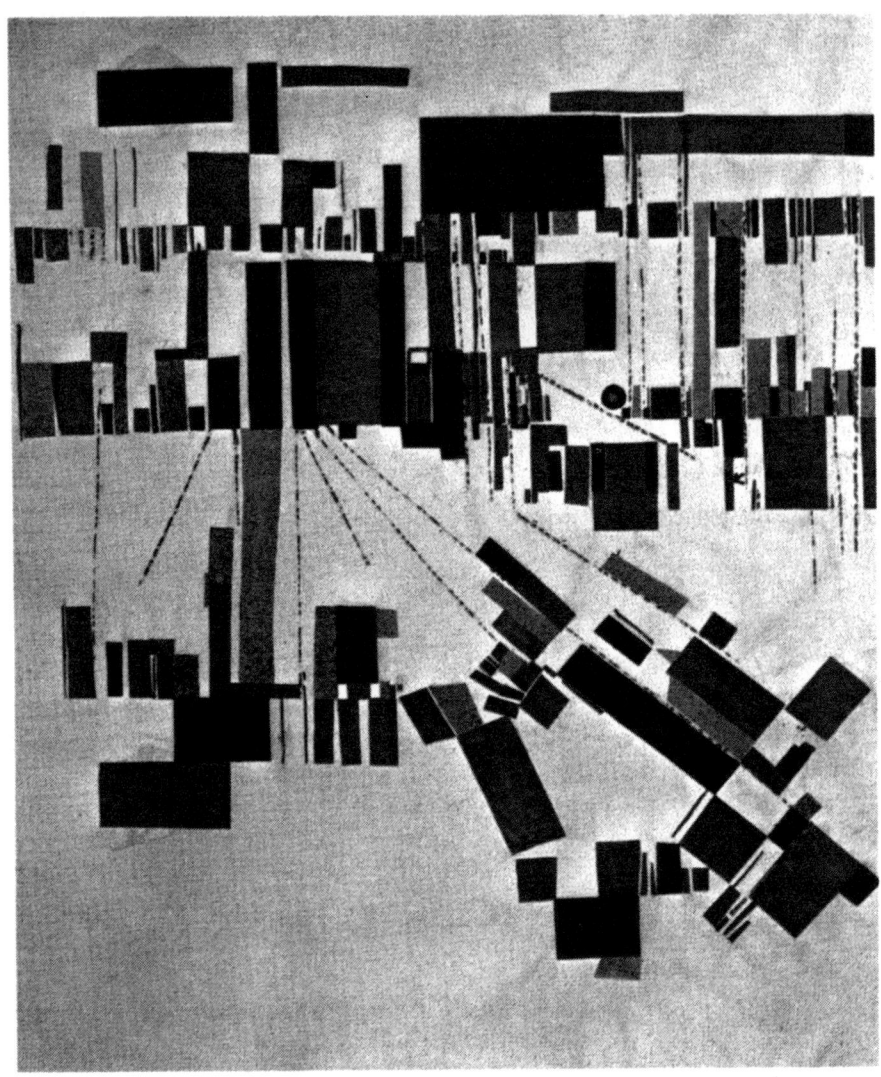

Hilla Rebay, *Credo*, 1949, collage, 19 x 23 in., included in "Homage to Hilla Rebay" exhibition.

Chapter XVII

Summing Up: "Skunkses is Skunkses"

I've heard people fighting over words for forty years. More than forty years. Whether or not a modern painting has depth and what its meaning is. They use terms like shallow depth, picture plane, color field. For me the important things in art are rhythm, balance, harmony, organization, the esthetics of space.

I don't talk about *depth*. What's that got to do with anything? I'd start at the foundation of all my reasoning, right back to Rudolf Bauer. Bauer doesn't have depth. He has *infinity*.

I'd happily dismiss many of the modern painters. If I were teaching art history, I would say they have made a fetish out of the conception of depth. This does not necessarily produce bad art. But it's idle to make the major criterion of a painting whether it has "depth" or not. It's all just words. Like mysticism. What do painters mean by mysticism?

Critics are always looking for inner meanings. They say Kandinsky was a theosophist. Fine. But to me Kandinsky's greatest weakness was that he spent so much effort trying to explain his metaphysical uncertainties and speculations. They call this mysticism. Everyone thinks they have the true word and if you don't agree, you don't really understand. I have always thought human intelligence is greatly undermined by people with the true word, like religious fanatics.

People looking at the paintings of Bauer and Kandinsky who don't understand and don't want to be thought of as dummies think they need some kind of explanation. I never wasted time defending any non-objective painting. They speak for themselves and have proven themselves. But Rebay was always defending her position. That was one of her faults. She was the same age I was and had painted as long as I had. She knew esthetic values perfectly well, yet she could not explain them.

Critics have to read in meanings and obscure ideas. There never has been any love lost between artists and critics. Critics do make people aware that the paintings exist, but a better way would be for cooperation between the artist, the dealer, and the critic. Whistler used to say that only artists can criticize art. But critics "make" the artists, and that's the sad truth.

A lot has been written about Jackson Pollock's career and how his wife Lee promoted his work. Peggy Guggenheim in her book *Art of This Century* gives credit for putting him over to J.J. Sweeney, and Clement Greenberg was also part of that clique. (*Greenberg did become a promoter for Peggy's young Americans n his writing.*)

Non-objective art, the geometric as well as the lyrical, continues to be created in this country despite all the efforts to stamp it out. My work, for example, has continued to be accepted, and sometimes I've been invited to show in juried exhibitions in museums across this country. Even the Metropolitan Museum, under great pressure from contemporary artists, finally had a show of modern work in 1950, including abstract and non-objective. and included one of my paintings which was reproduced in the catalogue. Later, a photograph of that painting was included an example of excellence in a book on composition.

If I could just get those paintings, mine and Bauer's and Rebay's and Kandinsky's (*Kandinsky should not be included in this diatribe; his paintings have been continually featured at the Guggenheim Museum*) and all the rest out of the Guggenheim's damned basement [warehouse] for one month, then we'd see. There are so many, more than sixty of mine alone and Lord knows how many Bauers. Let the public see them again. Let them decide for themselves if the wonder of it all is as I remember from long ago.

And what about me now? I'm ninety-three years old and I'm still painting and teaching. In January, 1982, I will have a show at the Washburn Gallery in New York City, all geometrics and non-objectives I did in the forties. Another bit of evidence that non-objective painting is still of interest to the world.

Of course this book has taken up a good bit of my time. I really didn't want to write it, and if I hadn't been born a blabbermouth I wouldn't have. Over the years I have always managed to get into these fat-chewing confabs at some gathering or other and somehow it would come out that I was a painter, and worse still a non-objective painter. So, before I would know what I was in for there would be questions about this and that in the art world. I would try to answer as simply as possible, and soon I would notice I had an audience. So more questions would follow and I would find myself being drawn out, often not happily, because frequently my answers were opposite the opinions of my listeners. I would always insist my point of view was the correct one, and then there would be needling remarks. "Then why don't you write the story of all these historical facts?" Or, "You have to get busy and write all this up." In a weak moment, just to get myself off the hook, I agreed. So here I am.

I have waited many years to hear or read a true account of the movement and the history of the museum, but no one has spoken and no one I have met has the slightest idea of the background of non-objective art in this country. I live in one of the most widely recognized art communities in the country [Woodstock, in upstate New York]. It has world-wide recognition. Yet I am constantly flabbergasted at the complete ignorance of the facts regarding the Guggenheim Museum as I meet and talk to the people in this town. They seem to hold the opinion that the Guggenheim Museum and Foundation and the non-objective movement in America "just growed" like Topsy without any outside help at all, and then quietly died a natural death. It didn't.

Maybe if this were an art movement that was definitely over, I wouldn't bother. But it isn't. I believe it is just starting.

For some reason, people who dislike or misunderstand Non-objective painting feel obliged to strike out against it. People who dislike a certain kind of music don't listen to it. If they dislike a writer they don't read him. But when it comes to art there are few silent dissenters — they scream out their objections. But Non-objective art isn't gone. And the fact that it is criticized, or belittled, or hidden, or called by another name doesn't change a thing.

It used to be that critics trying to explain non-objective painting would pass it off as just a mathematical formula or design. They arrived at that conclusion because they saw frequent use of geometrical forms and austerity of organization. But if non-objective painting was based on anything as simple as formulas or abstracted nature, it would have died years ago. It should be remembered that non-objectivism is one of the oldest "isms" of modern art, and today it is the most vigorous of any of them. The surface has merely been scratched.

I wonder what Rebay would think of this book. She'd probably take a look at it and say, "Scarlett, Scarlett, put your comma there. Don't put your period there. Don't run your sentence off the page like that. Change that word." And I'd say, "Of course, Baroness. You're quite right, Baroness."

In the old days when Rebay wanted to express her contempt for people who got in her way and fought her plans to advance non-objective art, she used to say in her German accent, "Scarlett, dirty Skunkses is vat they are! Skunkses is skunkses."

She lived long enough to see the movement well-launched with a promising future. But at the end of her life it was buried in the mud by the "Dirty Skunkses at the Museum."

Epilogue

Meeting Lyonel Feininger

Once, at one of the afternoon teas, I was admiring several Feininger watercolors when the Baroness walked over with Feininger himself. She greeted me as always and introduced us. "This is Rolph Scarlett, my great find. He is one of the best and his paintings will be placed in the company of Kandinsky's and Bauer's when the new museum is built. Tell me, Mr. Feininger," she went on, "when are you going to leave the world of realism and concentrate on non-objective painting?"

Feininger looked stricken. "But Hilla, how could I live without my world?" he said. You see that's the way he was. He could distort reality but couldn't create things unless there was some three-dimensional object to work from.

"You have painted those little boats. But if you take the triangular shapes you've used for the sails and cut them loose you'll be into the free geometric elements of non-objectivity."

"But, Hilla, I couldn't paint anything if I couldn't see it."

While the work of Rebay, Scarlett, and Bauer have largely disappeared from the history of art, Feininger's work has achieved world-wide recognition, selling at auction at Christie's in 2001 for more than three million dollars.

Hilla Rebay and Solomon R. Guggenheim

In 1927 Hilla Rebay arrived on the New York art scene with a letter of introduction to Solomon Guggenheim from his sister-in-law. That was his glory or his undoing. (*Other published material reports Guggenheim first meeting Rebay in 1925 in Berlin.*)

Solomon Guggenheim was a gentleman and had a great love for the fine things in life. Rebay was thirty-six years old when she met Solomon Guggenheim, who was then sixty-six years old. She was a vivacious redhead, an established painter and absolutely committed to non-objective art. To her it was a holy cause. If I had been as old as he was and met anyone as full of life and beauty and sex appeal as the Baroness Hilla von Rebay, I'd have lost my head too. Within two weeks she was on his yacht sailing up the Hudson. Two weeks later she was painting his portrait. From that moment on he was sunk as far as Non-objective painting was concerned. He would have given her anything she wanted and she wanted her religion spread. So with Rebay's drive and ambition and Sol's money behind it, the non-objective movement in America spread.

Rebay spent a lot of time with Mr. Guggenheim. They would often give afternoon teas at his apartment in the Plaza Hotel with Rebay usually acting as hostess to the group of artists who gathered there. I frequently attended these affairs and met many well-known European painters who had fled Hitler's advance.

The teas were held regularly every two weeks. From thirty-five to seventy-five people would attend and Rebay would always have a big spread. Trays of beautifully arranged sandwiches of various kinds and unique sweets and chocolates and wines of all kinds were ordered from the kitchen of the Plaza Hotel.

Many important people from the old Weimar Republic who were friends of Rebay and her family were invited. All the artists who possibly could would come and spend a very pleasant afternoon hobnobbing with European aristocracy and Sol would pay the bill and Rebay was very happy.

Sol's apartment *(shared with his wife Irene)* was in the Plaza Hotel, and he and Rebay had a lovenest in the Essex Hotel just down the street [on Central Park South]. Once Rebay called me to come and see her, as she did so often. When I walked in, she was sitting on the sofa crying. She came rushing over and threw herself in my arms sobbing. "Oh, that mean man, that mean man. I hate that little man." I guess they had had some kind of spat, which was not surprising considering Rebay's temperament. I was consoling her as best I could and trying not to get too involved when the door opened and in came Sol. He had forgotten his hat. He didn't say anything, just grabbed his hat and left. He probably didn't want to be seen by me.

What a tangled web it all is. Someone asked me once if it was true that Rebay had been Sol's mistress. Of course she had. I visited them often at the apartment in the Plaza Hotel where she acted as hostess for his afternoon teas, and on Sol's yacht where they often met, and in their Essex Hotel hideaway. Furthermore it was fairly common knowledge that she had been Bauer's mistress years before in Berlin. (*And that she had a short relationship with Kandinsky before that as well as with Hans Arp, who had introduced her to both Kandinsky and Bauer.*)

So the lives of these three people [Rebay, Guggenheim, and Bauer] were interwoven in more ways than one.

The tragedy is that because of this aspect of their lives, and the hate and resentment it caused, the great work to which they had devoted themselves in the art world was destined to be undone. The Museum at the center of the non-objective movement in this country falsified or destroyed the records of its beginnings. And the entire non-objective movement in this country was all but wiped out of our history.

Here one can only speculate as to why the Guggenheims hated and rejected Rebay and the artists who were her protegées. Kandinsky had a unique reputation on his own, which would explain how he avoided the exclusion, but the others all came into the [original] museum through Hilla.

The missing explanation which neither Scarlett nor Rebay ever mentions as to why she was "ousted" from the museum may well be the deep hatred and resentment Solomon Guggenheim's daughters (two of whom were on the Board) and his nephew, Harry (Board chairman), must have had for Rebay and probably Solomon too. His wife Irene, from the prestigious Rothschild family, was in her fifties when the affair between Sol and Hilla started and continued openly, flouting convention until Sol's death. There was never any formal separation from his wife, and Sol continued to entertain the artists whose works he collected at regular Sunday afternoon gatherings in the apartment he shared with his wife at the Plaza Hotel with Hilla acting as his hostess. Although never mentioned, it can be assumed that Irene was also present at these parties.

In a passage from Peggy Guggenheim's book Out of This Century *she describes visiting her Aunt Irene, Guggenheim's wife, in their apartment at the Plaza Hotel in the early 1940s — the same period as the glittering parties hosted by Rebay were taking place. "There existed at the Plaza Hotel a really fine collection of modern paintings owned by my uncle, Solomon, but accessible to the public only by special invitation. Aunt Irene lived there with my uncle surrounded by the most beautiful Picassos, Seurats, Braques, Klees, and Kandinskys. I told my aunt to burn all the Bauers [in the museum's collection] and move these paintings to the museum. She said, 'Shush! Don't let your uncle hear that. He has invested a fortune in Bauer.'"*

Irene was not only displeased with Sol's infatuation with Hilla but also did not understand his equally mad venture into collecting Non-objective art. Sol tried to explain that he had been a pioneer all his life. First in Mexico prospecting for mines, then in Alaska and Chile, always seeking new ore deposits. Now he was a pioneer and prospector in the new art. Irene understood this explanation as a rejection not only of her but also of her collection of old masters. Hilla and her Non-objective art was a new world for Sol and Irene was relegated to the sidelines.

*Hilla was totally devoted to art — it was her life as well as her religion. After she took charge of Sol's life and money, he too became passionately dedicated to art—and to the Non-objective artists she brought him. (His conversion is said to have happened after seeing a watercolor by Bauer.) But Hilla also gave him something that had eluded him until then — fame. Although an established mogul, it was the creation of the Solomon R. Guggenheim Art Foundation; the exhibitions organized by Hilla in his native city, Philadelphia, in 1937, in his winter residency city, Charleston, in 1938, and in his daughter Barbara's adopted city, Baltimore, in 1939; and the opening of the Museum of Non-objective Art in 1939 that finally gave Solomon R. Guggenheim world renown. The press celebrated him for his pioneering foray into modern art and for giving the American public its first **exposure*** *to contemporary European Non-objective painting. By 1939 Hilla had persuaded Sol to buy up almost every promising Non-objective painter in Europe adding to his collection 50 Kandinskys, 15 Gleizes, 6 Legers, 5 Moholy-Nagys, 3 Chagalls, 4 Delaunays, 2 Feiningers and all of Bauer's works. Six months before Mr. Guggenheim died at the age of 88 in 1949, he wrote:*

> Pioneering always attracted my attention as an advance, through contribution to the increase of mankind's material and cultural wealth. . . . The first time I saw a Non-objective painting in Europe, I was enchanted by its appeal and saw in this art a medium for the American painter to exceed the past. . . . In spite of much misunderstanding and almost discouraging advice I created a large collection of such paintings and have never regretted my intuitive decision nor my great faith in this art, as it grew on one, and I enlisted others to share my joy.

Portrait of Rolph Scarlett photographed by Harriet Tannin, 1980.

Chronology
Rolph Scarlett (1889-1984)

1889	Born June 13, 1889 in Guelph, Ontario, Canada. His father works as a cabinetmaker for the Bell Organ Co.
1901	Sister Antoinette, head of the Loretto Academy, learns about Scarlett's talents and tutors him in painting for one year.
1902	Graduates from St. George Academy. Apprenticed to W.A.Clark, a jewelry firm owned by his uncle.
1908	He and his friend Bruce Metcalfe leave Canada to vacation in the U.S.A. Vacation trip to New York City becomes a four-year residency.
1912	Returns to Guelph. Writes, directs, and produces musical and theatrical productions with Bruce Metcalfe.
1914	Writes and directs a musical comedy "The Gay Pierrots" based on the life of the suffragette Lydia Pinkham.
1916	Works for Massey Ferguson, Toronto, on shell production, until the end of World War I.
1918	Moves permanently to the U.S.A.
1919	Executive at Omega Watch Company.
1923	Travels to Switzerland. Meets Paul Klee and is introduced to abstract art.
1926	Moves to Toledo, Ohio. Exhibits abstract paintings in the Toledo Museum of Art (also in 1927 and 1928). Wins the Mohr Prize for his abstract painting. This is the first time an abstract painting is exhibited in Toledo and the first time an abstract painting wins a prize. Joins the Art Klan Group. Does stage design in theater groups where he meets his future wife, Emily Smith. She has two daughters, Barbara and Elizabeth Pollet, from a former marriage to artist Joseph Pollet.
1928	Moves to Hollywood, California. Works in movie studios as a scenery designer.
1929	Directs, choreographs, and designs sets for Bernard Shaw's *Man and Superman* for Pasadena Playhouse, California.
1930	Solo Exhibition, *Rolph Scarlett*, Hagemeyer Studio, Pasadena.
1932	Moves back to Guelph to paint full time.
1935	Returns to New York and works for Design Associates.
1937	Invents a target guided missile; his drawings are presented to the War Department in England. Files for a patent in same year. His oil painting *Composition* is bought by Hilla Rebay and Solomon R. Guggenheim for the Museum of Non-objective Painting, which is to open in 1939. More than 65 paintings, monoprints, and drawings for the museum's permanent collection are acquired for the collection in the next few years.

1939	Included in exhibitions at the Museum of Non-objective Painting on a regular basis until 1952. Begins Sunday lectures at the museum and is awarded a scholarship by the Museum's Foundation of studio space on the premises. Exhibits in Group Show, Golden Gate Museum, San Francisco, California.
1940	Group Show, *Realités Nouvelle*, Galerie Charpentier, Paris.
1945	Group Show, Modern Age Art Gallery, New York.
1947	Group Show, *Deuxième Salon des Realités Nouvelle*, Palais des Beaux-Arts, Paris (also in 1948).
1948	Group Show, *Society for Contemporary Art Exhibition*, Art Institute of Chicago; and at the University of Nebraska.
1949	Group Show, *Annual Exhibition of Contemporary American Painting*, University of Illinois. Solo Exhibition, *Rolph Scarlett*, Jacques Seligmann Gallery, New York.
1950	Group Show, *American Painting Today*, Metropolitan Museum of Art, New York.
1951	Group Show, *Annual Exhibition of Contemporary American Painting*, Whitney Museum of American Art, New York. Solo Exhibition, *Rolph Scarlett*, Illinois State College.
1953	Solo Exhibition, *Rolph Scarlett*, Jacques Seligmann Gallery, New York.
1955	Solo Exhibition, *Twenty Non-objective Watercolors*, Studio Guild.
1971	Group Show, *Non-objective Paintings*, Munson-Williams-Proctor Institute, NY.
1977	Group Show, *Visitors, Exiles and Residents*, University of Guelph, Ontario, Canada.
1980	Group Show, Zabriskie Gallery, NYC.
1982	Solo Exhibition, *Rolph Scarlett: Works from the 1940s*, Washburn Gallery, NYC.
1983	Solo Exhibition, *Rolph Scarlett: Drawings and Watercolors*, Washburn Gallery, NYC. Group Show, *Abstract Painting and Sculpture in America: 1927-1944*, Museum of Art, Carnegie Institute, Pittsburgh, Pennsylvania; exhibit travels to the San Francisco Museum of Modern Art, The Minneapolis Institute of Art, and the Whitney Museum of American Art.
1984	Dies in Woodstock, NY.
1987	Solo Exhibition, Associated American Artists, NYC. Group Show, *American Modernism*, The Ebsworth Collection, St. Louis Art Museum; exhibit travels to the Museum of Art, Boston and Honolulu Academy of Fine Arts.

1988	Group Show, *Foundations of the American Avant-Garde*, Struve Gallery, Chicago.
	Group Show, *American Abstract Drawing 1930-1987*, Arkansas Art Center, Little Rock.
	Three-person Show, *Rudolf Bauer, Rolph Scarlett, Hilla Rebay*, Sid Deutsch Gallery, NYC.
1989	Four-person Show, *In Review: Bolotowsky, Mason, Scarlett, Shaw*, Washburn Gallery, NYC.
	Solo Exhibition, Struve Gallery, Chicago.
	Group Show, *Masters of Geometric Abstraction*, Beth Urdang Gallery, Boston.
	Solo Exhibition, *Rolph Scarlett: Designs for the Theater*, Stubbs Books and Prints, NYC.
	Solo Exhibition, *Rolph Scarlett*, Struve Gallery, Chicago.
1991	Solo Exhibition, *Rolph Scarlett*, Schoelkopf, NYC.
	Group Show, *The Second Wave: American Abstractionists of the 1930's and 1940's*, Worcester Art Museum, Worcester, Mass.; exhibit travels in 1992 to the Samuel P. Harn Museum, University of Florida, Gainsville and the Delaware Art Museum, Wilmington.
1992	Group Show, *Improvisation: Kandinsky and the American Avant Garde, 1912-1950*, Phillips Collection, Washington, D.C.; exhibit travels in 1993 to the Dayton Art Institute, Ohio; Terra Museum of American Art, Chicago, and the Amon Carter Museum, Fort Worth, Texas.
1993	Solo Exhibition, *Rolph Scarlett: Monoprints*, Hirschl and Adler, NYC.
	Solo Exhibition, *Rolph Scarlett: Early Master of the Non-objective*, Woodstock Artists Association, Woodstock, NY.
	Group Show, *The Uses of Geometry: Then and Now*, Gary Snyder Fine Art, NYC.
1994	Solo Exhibition, *Rolph Scarlett*, Washburn Gallery, NYC.
	Solo Exhibition, *Rolph Scarlett: Gouaches and Prints from the 1930's and 1940's*, Beth Urdang Gallery, Boston.
	Group Show, *On Paper: Abstraction in American Art*, Rosenfeld Fine Art, NYC.
1995	Group Show, *New York: Two Different Perspectives*, Beacon Hill Fine Arts, NYC.
	Group Show, *1937: American Abstract Art*, Gary Snyder Fine Art, NYC.
1996	Group Show, *Abstraction in the Twentieth Century*, Solomon R. Guggenheim Museum, NYC.
	Solo Exhibition, *The Museum of Non Objective Painting: American Abstract Art*, Gary Snyder Fine Art, NYC.

Group Show, *Abstraction Across America 1934-1946*, Rosenfeld Gallery, NYC.

Group Show, *Champions of Modernism*, Mary Washington College Gallery, NY.

1997 Group Show, *Singular Impressions: The Monotype in America*, National Museum of American Art, Smithsonian Institution, Washington, D.C.

Solo Exhibition, *Rolph Scarlett: Art, Design and Jewelry*, Canadian Embassy Gallery, Washington, D.C. (preview of touring exhibition organized by Macdonald Stewart Art Centre, Guelph, Canada).

Solo Exhibition, *Rolph Scarlett 1889-1984*, Fletcher Gallery, Woodstock, NY.

1998 Group Show, *Against All Odds: American Abstraction from the 1930s and 1940s*, David Findlay Jr. Fine Art, NYC.

1999 Group Show, *The American Century: Art and Culture 1900-1950*, Whitney Museum of American Art, NYC.

Group Show, *Americans and Expatriates: Non-objective Painting in America 1920-1950*, David Findlay Jr. Fine Art, NYC.

2000 Solo Exhibition, *Rolph Scarlett: Art Design and Jewelry*, Macdonald Stewart Art Center, Guelph, Canada; exhibition traveled to the Kelowna Art Gallery, Kelowna, British Columbia and the Montreal Museum of Fine Arts, Montreal, Canada.

2001 Group Show, *Abstract Expressionism: Expanding the Canon*, Gary Snyder Fine Art, NYC.

2002 Group Show, *Kindrid Spirits*, David Findlay Jr. Fine Art, NYC.

Solo Exhibition, *Rolph Scarlett: Abstract Expressionist Works from the 1940s and 1950s*, Fletcher Gallery, Woodstock, NY.

2003 Solo Exhibition, *Rolph Scarlett: Art, Design and Jewelry*, Montreal Museum of Fine Art, Canada.

About Harriet Tannin

Woodstock artist Harriet Tannin did not begin her career in art until she was almost forty. She returned to school and received her MFA from the State University of New York at New Paltz in 1974. After graduation one of her first projects was to visit 100 Woodstock artists and photograph them in their studios. Paintings with a feminist direction followed, complemented by her book *The History of Art by H.W. Janson with Harriet Tannin*. This book was a result of discovering that Janson had not included a single woman artist in his epic history of art. She collaged herself into his reproductions of famous paintings, poking fun at Janson. When she found a trove of vintage undergarments spanning 1880 to 1980, she photographed them on models in appropriate settings for an exhibition, *Bustles to Boxers*, funded by New York State Council on the Arts. A duplicate set of black and white prints were later hand-painted to add a vintage look to the photographs. At present she is cutting and weaving photographs of antique mannequins. These and the hand-painted photographs can be viewed at the John Stevenson Gallery in New York City. Harriet's paintings and photographs have been included in many museum and gallery exhibitions and are included in the permanent collection of the Samuel Dorsky Museum, New Paltz, New York, and the Woodstock Artists Association, Woodstock, New York.

In 1969 Harriet Tannin met the artist Rolph Scarlett. What began as a student-mentor relationship developed into a 15-year close association that changed the direction of both their lives. She photographed, cleaned and repaired hundreds of his works under his direction as well as spreading the gospel of the importance of Rolph Scarlett to galleries and museum directors including those at the Solomon R. Guggenheim Museum. Since there was no reference in any art history books to non-objective painting or the original non-objective museum Harriet spent years researching old magazine and newspaper articles to put together a chronology of Scarlett's life. After his death Harriet Tannin became executor of his art estate and devoted another 15 years introducing the name Rolph Scarlett to galleries and museums. The Joan Washburn Gallery was the first to recognize his importance with an exhibit in 1982. Based on a series of taped interviews with Scarlett over a 15-year period, Harriet finished the video "Who is Rolph Scarlett" in 1980. Next she collaborated with Scarlett to expand on his book of memoirs begun in the 1950s. His original title, *Skunkses is Skunkses*, was a reference to those in charge who altered the direction of the Museum of Non-objective Painting from Hilla Rebay and Solomon Guggenheim's original plans.

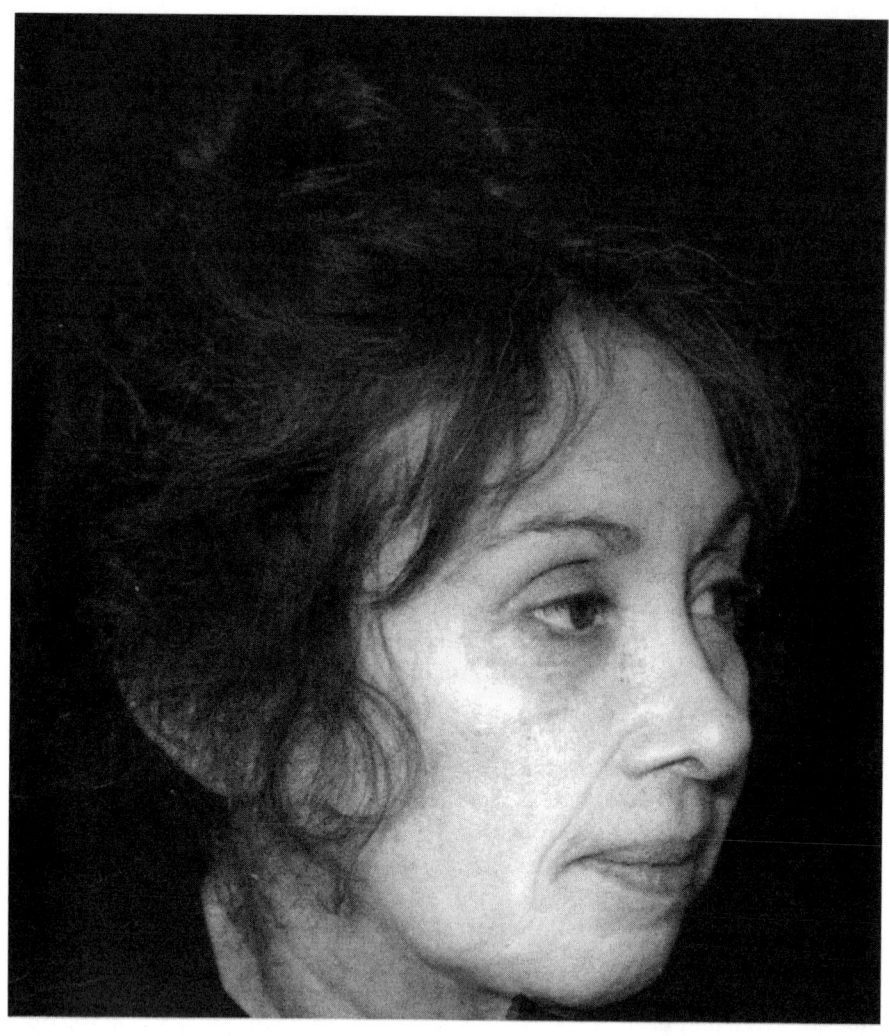

Harriet Tannin

Rolph Scarlett, *Composition*, 1938–39, oil on canvas, 31 x 53 in.; deassessioned by the Solomon R. Guggenheim Museum, 1996.

Rolph Scarlett, *Black Accent,* 1940, oil on canvas, 48 x 48 in.; private collection.

Rolph Scarlett, *Andante,* 1945, oil on canvas, 46 x 46 in.; Solomon R. Guggenheim collection.

Top:
Rolph Scarlett, *Untitled,* c.1945, gouache on paper,
8 1/8 x 12 5/8 in.; private collection.

Below:
Rolph Scarlett, *Untitled,* c.1945, gouache on paper,
9 x 11 1/2 in.; private collection.

Rolph Scarlett, *Red Form,* 1946, oil on canvas, 52 x 62 in.; private collection.

Rolph Scarlett, *Red Rugue,* 1940–47, oil on canvas, 54 x 54 in.; private collection.

Rudolph Bauer, *Spiritual Pleasures,* 1936.

Hilla Rebay, *Royally,* 1945.

Appendix

The following letters between Rolph Scarlett and Hilla Rebay are a sampling of their ongoing correspondence.

Great Neck, L.I. New York

April 4th, 1939

Dear Baroness,

"But the light, Mr. Scarlett, the light does not come from without; it is spiritual and comes from within; don't you see, from within." What a revelation to me those words were — "from within". Of course, of course. But that suggestion, like the many priceless ones which you have given me, is not just, a criticism, but an inspiration and stimulation, to help me towards the goal to which I have been so constantly though at times, aimlessly groping. Words of thanks are pretty futile return for such an illumination, we must look forward to the work which I hope to do to reward you and justify your belief in me.

I am full of gratitude to you for your unstinted encouragement, a gratitude which has been sharpened by years of arduous effort which met with little appreciation or success. Every true artist must travel the same lonely and painful road in his search for perfection. Rare and beautiful is it to meet someone like yourself to understand, encourage and inspire.

Once again, accept my poor thanks for being to me the inspiration you are.

With kindest regards, I remain,

Sincerely yours,

Rolph Scarlett

Franton Court
Greens Farms, Conn.
March 11, 1947

Dear Scarlett,

So it must be true, what the great Gabo told Mr. Guggenheim, and at his lecture in the Cincinatti Museum, that I was a great painter, because at last critics have attacked me — as no outstanding painter ever escaped vicious attack or to be maligned by those unable to grasp their message and who are involuntarily yet profoundly impressed by it, though unable to keep quiet about it.

I write to tell you, I like the painting with the green background as It is not imitating other painters' inventions and characteristics. Though it is a bit metallic again but is it deep enough? It seems to many that this you did too often and openly, as for Instance with Kandinsky, Bauer and Bertoia and others, and even If you found my new paintings exciting, I wish you would not use the way those last were done, with light background, as it was considered necessary to hide these paintings until I had brought them out In public first — before you could see them. But even then, it would be very much better <u>for you</u> if you developed Scarlett's own style. As long as you do not do this and also loosen your metallic painting technique, you cannot enter into the class of outstanding great personalities. Don't be too hasty, but try to raise your cultural knowledge. Read fine books and cultivate aesthetic relationships. Forget your erring intellect with which you detect other painters' painting but simply enjoy it and forget why, so that your own soul can speak when you paint. wish this for you — so much.

I wanted to make a colour reproduction of one of your paintings, but there was none I could find that did not remind me of another painter's influence or was entirely and only Scarlett. If you know better, which one is it?

P.S. Please write to me about it.
Now paint <u>slowly</u> and feel the space until you are properly guided from above.

With best wishes
your friend

MUSEUM OF NON-OBJECTIVE PAINTING
24 EAST 54TH STREET
NEW YORK CITY

HILLA REBAY
DIRECTOR

March 31st, 1947

My dear Friend Scarlett

It is not for being recognized by anyone that we must develop to become personalities; it is because each of us have another message to convey from above, and it is this above I want you to be reverent to, and not clutter your receivership by looking down to the messages already received. Since I was present, when you deciphered a Kandinsky water-colour, and I understood only then your handicap, I could see better how to help you out of intellectual hindrance. I want you to become loose from all this, and to develop up to receivership of that message, which you hindser coming through, and which is to be your own. Be simple; feel your space and forget that you ever saw a painting. Follow your inner need and let that be the speaker from above; be simple — be simple. And when you see a painting, enjoy it, simply, but do not take it apart. You have no gift of invention, that is just what I try to tell you. God is the only inventor. You have not learned your mental physics if you say so — and that is just your handicap.

You clutter yourself with thoughts and words and ideas you have heard, or read, or seen expressed by others, instead of feeling between the visionary inbetween. Some day you will understand me. Forget the whole world and feel your virgin space, be slow and don't think; let the higher ones guide your hand, but don't wait for it nor think about it, or even expect it. Do nothing but feel your space, enjoy its virgin beauty and just preserve its life in reverence so as to not kill its infinity, especially not with metallic paint. Delicately and sensitively draw and paint. Also with water-colors (*not* tempera) to develop transparency, and preserve this transparency of the space, but forget that any painting at all was ever done before by anyone. The resulting mastery is always a result of complete devotion to the infinite of space in utter simplicity; so let intuitive reaction only inspire you to the next stroke. You have no other responsibility but to concentrate on quality. Remember it is God who paints; <u>we are not doing it</u>, and this is what you must realize. If so, you will be most enriched and so will we be.

Aesthetics you find in the flight of a bird, in sunshine, in flowers' unfolding movements, in the beauty of lines, in graceful movements of any kind, in lovely thoughtfulness and deeds. You find it anywhere, once you are akin to its refinement — and more and more so, as you grow. Even the diamond needs a polish and rough handling so as to bring out its shine. So do we. Polish your tunnel, and the message will shine through soon enough and bring blessings.

Since I love nothing more than to enjoy such messages, it may be selfish if I expect so much of you. You have many friends besides myself Scarlett. Yet I hope you understand why I may be the only one, who takes the trouble of polishing — it is because I like the diamond not to be rough but to shine. And this you will!

As ever, sincerely

Hilla Rebay

MUSEUM OF NON-OBJECTIVE PAINTING
1071 FIFTH AVENUE
BETWEEN 88TH AND 89TH STREETS
NEW YORK 28, N.Y.

HILLA REBAY
DIRECTOR

November 1, 1948

Mr. Rolf Scarlett
32 Grace Avenue
Great Neck, L. I.

Dear Mr. Scarlett:

Naturally old Kandinskys, old Bauers, old Rebays, go out of the frame. Still since it was we who started before 1914 to develop this art expression, who had to study and establish the counterpointical discoveries which we presented to you on an easy silver platter when you first brought to me your decorations. Not one of your paintings even before that time goes out of the frame, and if you do it deliberately, so it must be so as to make it easy for yourself, which indeed it is.

When people write letters and use too large a script, they need many sheets of paper — there is so little they can say on one. Your far too large forms for a given space have the same result — and so on. But if it had not been for Miss Naess, who was dismissed, I would not even have been honoured with an answer; this is evident as you would riot have had to wait, and since you do not know facts about Miss Naess' dismissal, who acted very strangely, and fulfilled her duties very much to her own convenience. You need not give us advice. I have watched her for years, even when she was to supervise the mezzanine, she was never off her comfortable chair at the desk and anyone could have damaged paintings at the street side.

She even introduced a five day schedule for six days' pay, admitted it to Mr. Cohen, and told me an untruth by denying it. She brought strange people in my bedroom when I was absent, she wanted to use my personal addresses without asking me. She wasted her time in our office where she had no business to be, she never even came to the second floor of our exhibit, yet pretended to be a supervisor.

Money was constantly stolen but she now claims she left $20. in a drawer which was never found, and she was responsible for leaving it openly there for anyone to take, so she says. And so on, so on — this is a wonderful hostess indeed.

Hot air is not what we need but real and thorough devotion for a great cause of which people like yourself have derived benefit no end — although we never hear from you unless we <u>ask</u> or we can be useful in a way, please stay more in contact with your friends.

Sincerely,

Hilla Rebay

P.S. I see you opened a school congratulations and may God bless you and it only <u>please</u> do not harm our cause and get carried away — there is <u>so</u> much you know little, if anything about, specially avoiding *la qualité de la décoration, and la peinture* (the quality of painting itself) and falling for dealers' <u>demands</u> this is the end and of all people Seligman who should be dealing shoes—

FRANTON COURT
GREENS FARMS
CONNECTICUT

April 20th 1949

Mr. Rolph Scarlett
32 Grace Avenue
Great Neck, L.I., N.Y.

Dear Mr. Scarlett:

Miss Rebay directs that I write you in reply to your letter of April 7th, reminding you that she gave you practically all winter, asking you to contact her, but you failed to do so. Now that Mr. Guggenheim has returned to the City, she is extremely busy, and the visit you suggest cannot be arranged, at this time.

She also said how much she regrets it, as one of your paintings in our present show is so completely inartistic that it proves that you did not understand her advice at all.

Yours very truly,

L. Efros, Sec'y
to Hilla Rebay

From Rolph Scarlett, February 10, 1949

Dear Baroness,

I am so pleased that you called me sunday, and that all the petty little differences between us have been washed away.

I know very well that it is nothing but your interest in me, and what I am doing, that prompts you to give your time and trouble to help me with my painting..

Truthfully, I am most grateful for it, in spite of my petulant growling

From my experience with you in the past, I know how generous you have always been in your attitude towards painters who are striving to express themselves non-objectively. Therefore I naturally encourage the people that work with me to work hard, so that there might be a possibility of, at least having one painting hung in an exhibition at the Museum. Where else can these converts go?

Certainly no one knows better than you, even in a small way, the psychological boost of such recognition. These people through their enthusiastic conviction, are doing their utmost to contribute to the growth of the movement.

A small way, possibly, but nevertheless a sincere one. Best wishes and sincere regards,

New York
February 10, 1949

Museum of Non-Objective Painting
1071 FIFTH AVENUE
BETWEEN 88TH AND 89TH STREETS
NEW YORK 28, N.Y.

HILLA REBAY
DIRECTOR

January 16th, 1950

Mr. Rolph Scarlett
32 Grace Avenue
Great Neck, Long Island
New York

Dear Mr. Scarlett:

The collection of paintings which includes also some of your works, and which we sent in 1947 to France, and upon invitation from there to Switzerland, and again from there to German Museums, was ready to be returned now from Bremerhaven to New York, December 17th. A cable requested our consent that exhibit is taken over by the American authorities, so that once again it can be shown in all the America Houses of all larger cities of Germany. Since you had given permission to exhibit your work further on, I consented. I hope this will show you how effective our show has been. And you probably will also be pleased that this is a proof that non-objectivity is becoming officially represented by our own government due to the great interest there, and praise we received, over press and radio and again, at each different opening.

This, I feel, is an accomplishment and a gratification for the pioneering work, which I did in the last several years over there with artists and historians of art in many prominent art centers of Europe. In making a name for American art in Europe and especially in Germany, known as the foremost historical research center which so established all good painters only through their serious interest, can give a lasting historical stamp to non-objectivity, impressive to American historians, as has already been done. This, of course, is also to your interest. So I feel certain that continued cooperation is beneficial to all who have participated in this show, and that my unending work of promoting others and the Art is beginning to bear ever-increasing results.

Sincerely,

Hilla Rebay

MUSEUM OF NON-OBJECTIVE PAINTING
1071 FIFTH AVENUE
BETWEEN 88TH AND 89TH STREETS
NEW YORK 28, N.Y.

HILLA REBAY
DIRECTOR

February 28, 1951

Mr. Rolph Scarlett
32 Grace Avenue
Great Neck, Long Island, N.Y.

Dear Mr. Scarlett:

Of course, I would be very glad to see you and talk with you again about your painting; but do you think that this would be of any avail, and would you truly believe what I might advise? If you have faith and respect for my opinions and suggestions, why do you still in your paintings extend your forms out of the given space — which, as you know, is one of the most serious faults of composition, and which certainly cannot add to your satisfaction.

Your painting in the Metropolitan Show has the same contrapuntal mistake, and had you listened to me it could have been ever so much better. There are other points I would very much like to tell you — but only if you feel, and eventually show that it will have any effect. Somehow, I have the feeling that you prefer to believe others rather than heed my experienced advice.

Why don't you come out to Greens Farms some Sunday when both you and I would have time to discuss your work more fully? It is such a pity that you do not develop yourself as you go along. I find that you derive your inspiration from other persons' more or less poor techniques and superficial mannerisms, and you thereby cloud your own fine ability by mere imitation, instead of expressing your own inner soul, your own individual personality, your personal feelings, into action by responding to the given space and virgin white purity with unadulterated beauty. This latter effort should be your expression toward the goal you wish to achieve.

My telephone number is FAIRFIELD 9-0572 (Connecticut). If you wish, you may call me there some evening, so we can arrange to get together.

You can well imagine how very much I am interested to see you continue to be one of our group, and to develop into that which I have for so long a time wished and hoped for you to become. As it is now with the present kind of output, you disqualify even the excellent things you have done in the past. Also, this factor has put me in a most embarrassing position — since naturally we cannot represent a painter who has been retrogressing rather than progressing in our future museum. As you know, there is a considerable investment in your paintings, so you can well understand the embarrassment of my position due to your lack of adherence to my advice for the enrichment and fulfillment of your inner self's expression.

I don't think I have to tell you how happy I would be were I able to write to you with my utmost conviction: "Dear Mr. Scarlett... I was so happy to see your beautiful new paintings, etc." — as nothing would give me greater joy than to see you growing in your work, attaining greater and greater heights.

With kind regards, I am

                                        Your friend

                                        Hilla Rebay

MUSEUM OF NON-OBJECTIVE PAINTING
1071 FIFTH AVENUE
BETWEEN 88TH AND 89TH STREETS
NEW YORK 28, N.Y.

HILLA REBAY
DIRECTOR

December 14, 1951

Dear Mr. Scarlett:

"To say the least" as you say in your letter, which seems to indicate a personal right to glory and righteousness, every word I would answer to your strange inquiries would be a waste of my precious time because it would again, and as it has been proven before, be totally out of your possibility of comprehension.

That you have had in me a true friend, perhaps you may still admit. I am afraid, however, that your understanding of me is at an end. The only thing I want to say to you is that I thought, you were a true seeker; a reverent artist in search of discovering the many possibilities of space beautification. But this, I was sorry to find and to see, was not your intention. Because it now seems that your painting was a means to a materialistic end; perhaps in line with your surroundings, of which to free your soul you were unable or unwilling, and which is killing the best in you in which I had believed. Instead of using your commercial abilities to give you independence in your artistic work, you wanted to receive practical benefits where only spiritual ones can be expected, although the miracle of selling non-objective paintings, which I never managed for myself (nor you for me), has been your share over and over again due I presume mostly to my unselfish help. And so you lent your ears and eye to everyone, if not anyone, whom you considered being in the limelight of commercial success. Even to the most ignorant dealer's stupid advice you listened more than to me, whom you stopped asking for advice. Your unhappiness increased, and you lost your way by denying faith and aping styles of others as fast as the chameleon changes colours. So your way ended in the horrid jungle it is in now; even a Mr. Pollock's smearage was not bad enough for you to have a try at; and betraying yourself, you betrayed art and my faith in you, and my present disgrace by my failure to foresee such an outrageous possibility — since you even paint objectively now, I am told, which may be true only of Mr. Pollock, which would be where he belongs.

So what have I to say to you is that I am utterly disgraced, and should take all Scarlett paintings out of the collection so that you can never claim hanging in the finest, noblest, sincerest, and spiritually most cultured museum in the world, considering the present state of your painting. There is an ideal we strive for, Mr. Scarlett. There is a monument to God we serve, Mr. Scarlett. There is a service we render twenty-four hours a day to others, Mr. Scarlett. There is a noble task to fulfill, Mr. Scarlett, and there is an obligation to follow, a deep reverent modesty to profess. There is a reverence to the creative spirit to serve. Which is all there is that matters, after which we see the material worries ending as they consequently do. As perfection is the Universe's embrace to all those, who live in its service; all our worry has to be, and is, that question; do we give enough and do we give as best we can. Dear Mr. Scarlett, not this question: what do I get out of it. Earthly things, anyone can get and give; to whom the higher, finer noble ingredients of the creator's essence do not matter. If you had refined your electrical body's receiving station with mental physics and your very self to such conception and intention, your material ends would have been taken care of automatically and there would be now a painter in existence who is a Scarlett, not a copyist of other people's clothing styles and personal handwriting, natural to them alone, and to no one else. And as you listen to any silly dealer's advice, you listen to those limping behind as nincompoops. Their level is so low that you have to sink down to reach it.

The artist of great personality refuses such low down measures since he is consecrated to a devotion aiming higher than himself. The only way to keep this service as pure, as fine, as noble as the infinity of eternity and perfection is, by searching its law in intuitive guidance, with help of an incredibly useful but demanding conscience, dear Mr. Scarlett. Only in the hardship of such service can there be benefits, success and happiness. In your present painting, if painting you may call it (I would call it smearage), you not only disgrace yourself but all those who trusted you and helped you and who had never thought possible the insult you dare to Mr. Guggenheim's noble faith and great monument by sending such accidental, uncontrolled, banal, incompetent and unesthetic work, lacking design, law, refinement, culture, space, definition. Also the creation of a spiritual dimension in precise, lawful, rythmic connecting relationship.

All I can say to you is this, if commercial glory is all you are after, forget about our existence and blame yourself for the misery. Were it not for your former good comradeship, you can rest assured, "to say the least," there would have been no answer to your letter. Since you know better. And you knew what you were doing, there is no excuse that you did not know. Is there a greater fool than the one who fools himself? That I hope you still can avoid and again find the way you have lost, the way to feel and follow the best in you. The only goal to express intuitively, not intellectually, and to satisfy or regain a demanding conscience, when you search for space beautification. Without the ways and means others may find necessary, and which you should never follow as God gives each of us a different way of saying what He wishes us to say. It is not you or I who express, it is always and only the "Non" which expresses creation through us, and which high intelligence people call God. As eternity which is now, we feel now, when we create we do not think of what is past and already done by others. May your further search direct your steps into a better lane and you will be blessed again.

HvR: b

                                        Sincerely,

                                        Hilla Rebay

Mr. Rolph Scarlett
c/o Swivellier Co. Inc.
30 Irving Place, New York, New York.

Letters and descriptions of Scarlett's missile design:

During the fall and winter of 1937-1938, Scarlett worked in London for the British War Office making drawings and specifications for a guided missile. In December 1937, Scarlett presented detailed drawings and specifications to the British Patent Office, London.

> "I submit the idea that an especially designed shell can be fired from an anti-aircraft gun and an attacking plane and at a certain pre-determined point, the shell can release a torpedo, or rocket torpedo, which is self-propelled and so designed and constructed that one of the animated forces of the plane will attract the rocket to it. In other words, within certain limits the rocket will follow the plane."

First letter addressed to the British Embassy describing his Target-Guided Missile proposal as described in Chapter II.

October 26, 1937

Col. W. W. Torr
Military Attache
British Embassy
Washington, D. C.

Dear Col. Torr:

    I hereby submit an idea which I believe can be highly effectively employed to combat airplane attacks. It is based on what I believe an entirely new method or philosophy of shooting or trajectory. The philosophy is based on the principle that the target governs the course of the projectile, rather than the source from which it is discharged.

    I am taking this matter up with you with the understanding that you will forward this communication to the War Office in London, where they will treat it with the utmost secrecy, a course which I have already followed, and I hereby give you my assurance that this has not been given to any other Power for its consideration. My reasons for doing this are several, probably the most important being that, while I at present live in the United States, I am a Canadian and would like to see the advantages of this idea go to the Mother Country first. Also, I believe the need for finding a means to successfully repel airplane attacks is very great indeed.

    From all the facts before me I am of the opinion that

projectiles of all sorts have always been discharged on the principle that the course of the projectile was governed by the source from which they were discharged. The distance covered, the degree of accuracy, etc., being subject to the size and kind of missile plus the means and efficiency of the weapon employed to discharge it. That principle, or philosophy, is as old as man and so long as the target was a mechanically inanimate object there was no means by which that old principle could be changed or improved. But there has been, to my mind, for some time now another and I believe a better way of achieving firing accuracy, assuming that the target is of a type that I call animated mechanism.

There are many weapons used in modern warfare, or rather there are many carriers of weapons, which are admittedly animated mechanisms. Such as all modern navy craft, including undersea vessels, land force pieces, such as armored trains, armored cars, tanks, etc., and air forces, such as airplanes and dirigibles. Admitting that these various weapons are animated and submitting here the principle that the animation of such weapons can be used to govern the course of a projectile I am presenting a principle that, when fully developed and used, will prove of incalculable value as a defensive weapon, and which might when ultimately applied, prove an offensive weapon of enormous potentialities.

At present, I have concentrated my thoughts with the possibility of using this principle solely as an effective means of repelling airplane attacks. So I submit the idea that especially designed shell can be fired from an antiaircraft gun at an attacking plane and that at a certain predetermined point the shell can release a torpedo, or rocket torpedo, which is self-propelled and so designed and constructed that one of the animated forces of the plane with attract the rocket to it and thus be destroyed by it. In other words, within certain limits, the rocket will follow the plane.

The rocket can be so effectively developed that it can achieve a very high degree of efficiency and that it can be made to reach an altitude which is way beyond the range of modern anti-aircraft weapons, or the possibilities of such weapons of the future. There is undoubtedly an enormous amount of research and experimentation to be gone through before this principle will be a success. <u>But where the need is great and where the necessary resources are available, all that remains is the determination to see it</u> through.

During the period I have spent researching and developing the ways to make it work I have formulated innumerable methods and have worked them out, on paper, and I am convinced that existing mechanical and scientific principles are already to hand which need only the consideration of various engineering minds to make one of the methods wholly successful. The logical way to submit this idea to the War Office undoubtedly would be to present as many of these plans as comprehensive for the War Office to use as a starting point. However, if the general idea of the principle seems reasonable, I would of course present myself to the proper authorities if and when desired.

I have not taken steps to seek a patent on the idea in any of the various forms that I have so far developed for the reason that I believe absolute secrecy is imperative. And the very process of applying for such patent would at once eliminate the element of secrecy. Furthermore, I again state that I have not divulged this idea to anyone and it is on the strength of your recommendation that I am pursuing this course in presenting this to the War Office.

I cannot help but feel that to submit only one idea, or a development of the idea, which may for many reasons not be the best one, is presenting it at a distinct disadvantage. To cover all the various questions that will necessarily arise by mail naturally would be completely unsatisfactory. The fact remains that if I could present my many solutions to the War Office a great deal of time would be saved and the feasibility of the idea much more easily accepted.

With regard to remuneration I would say that, although I have studied the Memorandum for Inventors, I do not see at present any basis for arriving at a definite payment. This can be worked out at some future date with the War Office after they have had the opportunity of studying the matter. Naturally should this idea have possibilities which I feel assured of, and should the War Office agree with me, I would expect transportation and expenses advanced to enable us to go to London to discuss the matter in detail.

I wish to take this opportunity to thank you for your kindness and cooperation.

Very sincerely yours,

Rolph Scarlett
32 Grace Avenue
Great Neck, L.I. New York

The initial description of the Target-Guided Missile submitted to the British Patent Office.

February 2, 1938

I submit herewith the principle for an invention for the destruction of aircraft. In this proposal I make use of the emanations of the aircraft to guide the missile which is approaching it, so that it will hit it. The missile, which, for the sake of argument, we may be supposed to be fired from a 4.7 anti-aircraft gun. It may be so shaped and arranged that having approached the target for some seconds as a projectile, by the action of a time fuse it may become a rocket, and thereafter proceed at an approximately uniform velocity under its own power. It will be noticed that whereas rockets which leave the ground as such, require to be especially light to enable them to get up into the air, in this case a combination of projectile-rocket, the rocket action comes into play when the trajectory is nearing the horizontal and is only required to maintain a velocity already imparted to a body; against the deceleration caused by the small vertical component of gravity and that caused by air resistance. Consequently the weight of the missile is less important.

The projectile will be fired 'with as much accuracy as an ordinary anti-aircraft projectile, so that it can be relied upon to come near enough to be sensitive to the emanations of the plane — the plane aimed at. A plane in motion sends off sound vibrations from the propellor, also another type of sound vibrations from the exhaust, also a magnetic field and also Herzian waves, due to the high tension sparking of the engine. While anyone of these emanations may be utilized it is preferred to make use of the Herzian waves as being the most instantaneous and continuous. The rocket may carry a direction detector which registers both the direction and the force of the emanation, and by actuating a guiding apparatus may steer the rocket into the plane. It will be appreciated that, whereas it could be exceedingly difficult if not impossible to change the direction of a projectile in flight, in the case of the rocket the problem is far easier. For here, all that is necessary is to change the orientation of the major axis of the rockets and direction of flight will be changed correspondingly, since the direction of the ejected gases is changed. It is also possible, through the use of valves placed at each side, placed forward or in the rear, (each side meaning all four sides), i. e., north, south, east and west, in the body of the rocket; to change the direction of the rocket by the use of exhaust gases being emitted as desired through any one of the various valves. I venture to submit that I now claim originality to new principles of fundamental importance. One, that it is possible to use a heavy rocket provided its velocity is initially imparted by a gun charge and Two, that we have in the rocket the ideal body whose direction can be easily changed during flight, on receipt of a signal from outside. Apart from the details of construction which follow, and even supposing no details followed, these two principles form the basis for experimentation which should prove of great value toward the solution of the problem.

METHOD USING SMOOTHE BORE GUN AND WIRELESS TELEGRAPHY, OR HERZ-IAN WAVES, EMANATIONS FROM AIRPLANES.

A gun of any calibre may be used sufficiently large to give room inside for rockets for the necessary working parts. It is here suggested that the gun 4.7 AA could be satisfactorily used. In the 4.7 AA gun, the inder tube is removed and an unrifled tube substituted. The projectile differs from an ordinary 4.7 AA projectile in that it is somewhat blunt-nosed and has four long steel rods projecting to the rear. See Diagram 1.) The projectile may also be made with four collapsible, or telescoping, fins, running lateral) the entire length of the rocket and extending to at least the full distance of the length of the rocket to the rear. These fins are so constructed mechanically as to fold flush with the periphery of the body of the rocket and remain in that position while being discharged from the gun. Put once in flight as a rocket, these fins may automatically be ejected from their respective recesses and so form the necessary veins to stabilize the course of the rocket in flight and prevent lag or sideslip.

We turn now to detailed description of the tail fins.

2,2 — which will normally take the position shon and are kept in the position shown dotted by its confining action while travelling down the bore. The fins, 2, are attached to rods, 1, by steel springs. The base of the rocket is sealed by a steel plug, 3, Diagram 1, which rests against a step, 4, in the body of the rocket. This plug takes the shock of discharge and carries in itself a time fuse which, after the number of seconds of flight to which it has been adjusted, performs three separate operations on explosion. A - it blows off the base plug by means of small powder charges, 5, suitably placed around the periphery of the plug. B — it ignites the rocket composition in the combustion chamber by means of a flash carried up a suitable channel, 6. C — it brings into action the detection and guiding apparatus in the head of the rocket, 9. The combustion chamber must be well in front of the center of gravity of the rocket and I show it at 7. In this model I propose the fuel for propulsion to be one of liquid oxygen and gasolene. It is desirable to store the fuel where it Is heated by the discharging gases, as shown in the compartment 8,8. It is estimated that these rockets should be capable of carrying this projectile at the uniform velocity of 1,000 FS to 2,500 FS, say for a distance of five miles or further.

It is here claimed that during the flight of the body as a projectile, there being no rotation due to rifling, the fins have to function to keep the projectile head-on in the direction of flight of the body as a projectile, and these same fins perform an analagous function while In the latter status the body is moving as a rocket. In order to avoid any distortion of these fins by the turbulent gases at the moment of leaving the gun muzzle, I suggest a reduced charge which will give a muzzle velocity of say 2,300 FS instead of the usual high velocity of perhaps 2,700 FS. By this sacrifice I insure the charge being fully burnt at the muzzle, and there will be no disturbing gases. The setting of the fuse may present some difficulty since it is enclosed within the brass cartridge case. A hole could be provided in the cartridge case and a special key for reaching the fuse could be provided. On the other hand, this latter precaution may not be necessary, because a predetermined setting of the time fuse could take care of this problem.

Rocket experience shows that all bodies behind the point of discharge of the gases become intensely heated. Consequently it would be unwise to rely on rudders for steering the rocket. I propose, therefore, to steer by means of a deflecting apparatus, 9, Diagram 1, in the nose of the rocket. This apparatus is also shown in detail in Diagram 2. It consists of a hollow cylinder, 10, mounted on roller bearings, coaxially with the rocket. The front end of this cylinder carries a hollow cup, 11, mounted as shown. The rolls, 13 and 14, of the cup are inclined outwards at an angle of 12 degrees, it being a favorable angle to impart lateral pressure from the rush of the gases. The cup consists of two halves, 13 and 14, each semi-circular in section and so arranged that when revolved on their axis one passes just inside the other.

It will be seen, then, that by rotating the axis of 13 and 14 suitably, we can create an aperture of any desired size or, alternately, close the circle. A device is contained inside the hollow cylinder and is indicated by 28 for operating this aperture, and is so arranged that both half cups are always simultaneously moved, but in opposite directions, so that however big the aperture its center remains at a given place relative to the hollow cylinder, 10. When, however, the cylinder itself is revolved, the aperture revolves with it. We have, then, a means of exerting force to change the direction of the axis of the rocket which can be varied both in direction and in degree. When the cup is closed it will be full of slightly compressed air, the overflow of which is flowing over the nose of the rocket. As soon as the aperture is opened, the air will escape on that side, thus exerting a force in the opposite direction to push the axis around, and since there is nothing gyroscopic about this non-spinning rocket, the axis will be deflected in that direction and the rocket will move in the new direction, (with a slight lag owing to inertia.) The more the aperture is opened the more swiftly will the axis of the rocket be pushed around and the more rapidly will the rocket change direction. It is obvious also that the direction of the change is controlled by revolving cylinder, 10.

The reprinting of the above initial description submitted to the British Patent Office is to document Scarlett's extraordinary proposal. There are several more pages of descriptions and diagrams which are not reprinted here.

The following is a response from the British War Office [?] regarding the redrafting of the description of the proposal submitted to the patent office.

14 Queens Gate Gardens,
S.W.7.

7th March, 1938.

My dear Scarlett,

You will see from the enclosed that the Patent Office were not satisfied with our application for patent.

I therefore redrafted our provisional application and sent it in draft form to the Patent Office.

I enclose a copy of their reply of the 4th March.

I have amended the redrafted application accordingly and send you the top copy and duplicate for signature at the end.

Please send them both back to me as soon as possible so that I may lodge them formally.

Yours sincerely,

Rolph Scarlett Esq.,
32 Grace Avenue
Great Neck, Long Island, U.S.A.

Tel. No.—Whitehall 9400.

Any further communication on this subject should be addressed to:—
The Under-Secretary of State,
The War Office,
London, S.W.1.
and the following number quoted.

84/Gen/8009 (M.G.O.(A).b.)

THE WAR OFFICE,
LONDON, S.W.1.

3rd November 1938

Dear Mr Scarlett

I am to refer to your letter dated 10th October 1938 and to return herewith as requested the drawings 11 sheets submitted by you on 1st December 1937

Yours truly,

W. A. Canter

Director of Scientific Research.

R. Scarlett Esq.

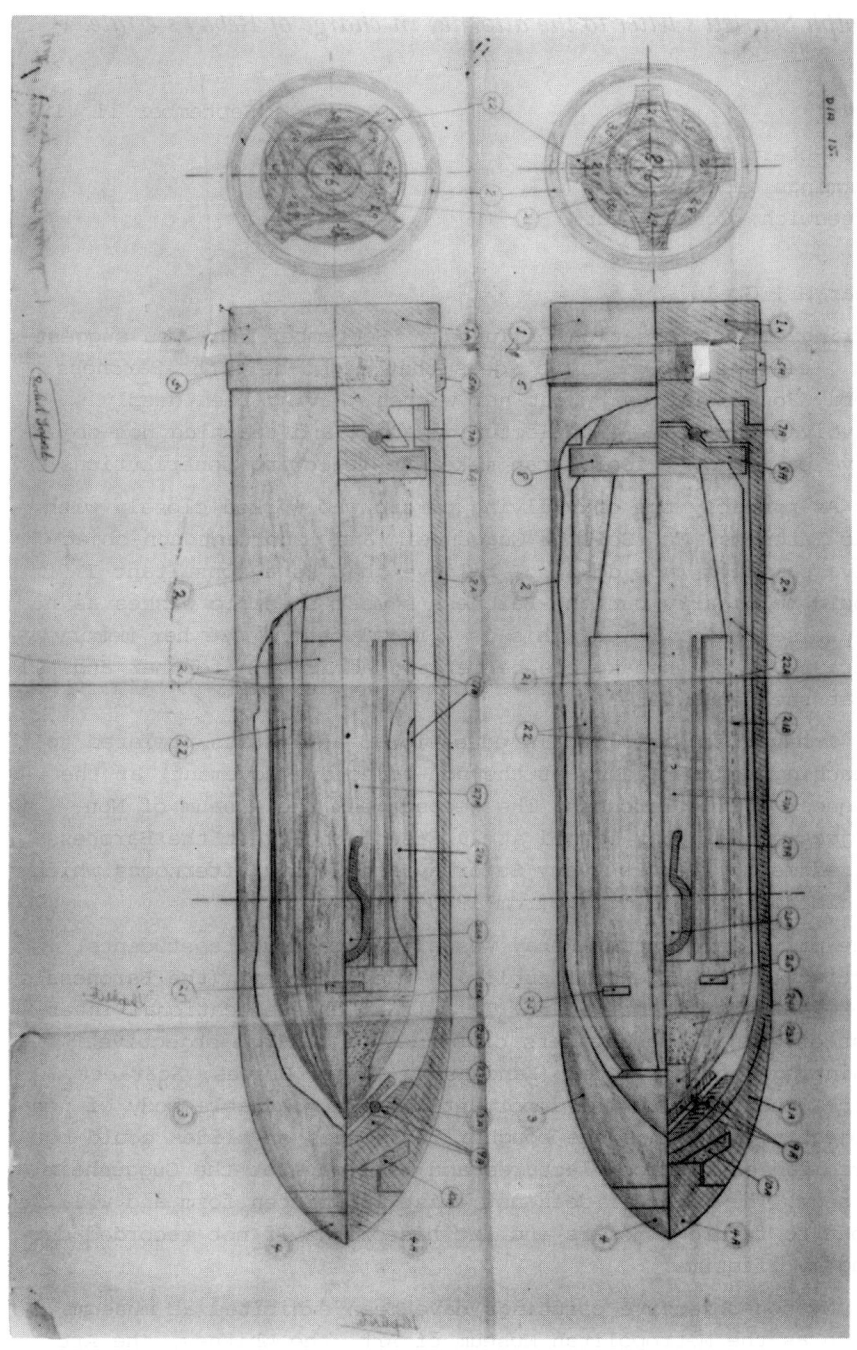

Scarlett's drawing for Guided Missile Design.

Rolph Scarlett's letter to the attorney in charge of Rebay's estate.

September 11, 1972

Mr. Robert Grele
Cummings and Lockwood
Greenwich, Connecticut

Dear Mr. Grele:

During our conversation of Tuesday, September 5th, you suggested I contact you if I had ideas that might help the Baroness Rebay Foundation carry out her wishes. Having been deeply involved for years with lecturing about and teaching non-objective painting, I feel I can make the following contributions:

1. As probably the only living person who worked closely with the Baroness, Mr. Solomon Guggenheim and important non-objective painters (now dead), I believe that as a consultant I could help carry out the Baroness's most specific wishes as no one else could. 1 feel this is a moral debt I owe her memory because of my unshakeable belief and admiration for her and all that she stood for.

2. I have been involved in educational activities (related to teaching and spreading of the non-objective movement) at the request of the Baroness. The second week the Museum of Non-Objective Painting opened at 29 East 54th Street the Baroness hired me to lecture every Saturday and Sunday afternoons which I did for 5 or 6 years, from 1940–1946.

The prime interest of Rebay was always to educate students, artists and the general public in the "glories" (the Baroness's term) of non-objective art. To fulfill this educational interest of hers I suggest sets of slides of the non-objective paintings she collected (Kandinsky, Bauer, Drewes, Scarlett, etc.) that make up the important and irreplaceable body of non-objective paintings she bought. These sets of slides could be accompanied by taped lectures and as I gave at the Guggenheim Museum. The material does not exist in written form and will be lost to future scholars and art historians If not recorded during my lifetime.

3. My non-objective paintings have been exhibited at museums such as the Metropolitan Museum of Art, the Whitney, the Art Institute of Chicago, University of Illinois, where I also lectured, and in museums across this country, Canada and Europe.

The Baroness believed in my work and was completely responsible for the purchase of 85 of my paintings now in the permanent collection of the Guggenheim Museum. Many colleges in this country are now collecting original works of art. Would the Foundation be interested in furthering this major interest of the Baroness (educating people to understand non-objective painting) by purchasing from me some non-objective paintings to donate to educational institutions such as the Rockefeller University, Harvard, Dartmouth, New York University, etc., in the Baroness's name? Accompanying each picture would be educational material explaining the picture.

4. Also of interest would be conversations I had. with the Barones at the beginning of the planning of the present Guggenheim Museum, and the meetings with Frank Lloyd Wright as to its location.

5. Xeroxed materials which show my status as a painter are enclosed.

I trust you will not consider me too presumptuous in offering these suggestions, but the rehabilitation of Miss Rebay is a matter dear to my heart, owing to my long relationship with her during those early years.

Also, her all-important contribution to the world of art should be given the recognition it deserves, and form part of the historical record for future generations. Only a person of fanatical dedication could have achieved what she did in stimulating the whole non-objective and abstract movement internationally.

I hope to hear from you in the near future,

Sincerely,

Rolph Scarlett

Review of Static from the Toledo Blade, *April 3, 1926 and a review of Scarlett's set designs for* Man and Superman *from* Star News *(Pasadena), 1929, as described in Chapter IV.*

APRIL 3, 1926 — TOLEDO BLADE

Precedent Established.

In accepting "Static," a painting by R. W. Scarlett, 519 Nicholas avenue, and giving it a place in the local exhibition, the exhibition judges established an almost revolutionary precedent.

Mr. Scarlett, an artist of the futurist school, submitted 18 examples of his work. "Static," an attempt in primary pastels to describe ocularly the blasting torments of the electrical interference which regularly assails the ears of radio enthusiasts, was accepted. In the history of the federation shows, it was the first futurist canvass submitted for exhibition and the first to be accepted.

And, being futurist, it was accepted only because no one has seen static. No means for judgement on a representative basis could be found.

SETTINGS WIN ATTENTION

Experiment at Playhouse Inspires Reviewer

'SCENE' 'ACTS' IN UNUSUAL EFFECT

By THE STAR-NEWS CRITIC

Shaw goes well at the Playhouse. Thursday night's brilliantly provocative experimental production of "Man and Superman" captured in the first three minutes after the rise of the curtain the surprised imaginative co-operation of an intelligently consenting house. Why not?

Ralph Scarlett, guest art director, trained in the values of expressionistic modern painting, finds running throughout the play one tremendous gripping theme. This is "the urge of the life force which uses any characters at any period of time or space to carry out its relentless purpose." He believes that the very brilliance of Shaw's dialogue obscures at times the hidden meaning of this paramount motif. And because reviewing space is always limited, and most people are by this time tolerant of the Shaw philosophy, it will be my purpose here to treat particularly of the means employed by Mr. Scarlet to highlight the pulse beat of this theme.

"Scene" Has Action

Borrowing from all the arts, architecture, music, ballet, we have an abstract constructive setting erected for each changing scene, to show not only the struggle of man's soul for self assertion in the grip of natural forces that control his emotions, but his confusion of mind amid the entangling mechanisms of modern civilization. The orchestra is composed of two motors, a drum, a flute and a saxophone. Back of the queer shapes and fantastic structures that entrap the characters, is the blue expanse of background against which in gigantic shadow is thrown the weaving dance of the interpretive ballet. Music, lighting, ballet, are all a living part of the action. The "scene" in Gordon Craig's expressive phrase "acts" almost as potently as the players.

Reviews of Scarlett's stage sets and painting exhibition in California newspapers.

LOS ANGELES, CAL., RECORD, NOVEMBER 19, 1929

SHAVIAN PLAY CLOSING RUN THIS WEEK

CAST GIVES DREAM SCENE OF PLAY

By THE STAR-NEWS CRITIC

Monday night began the third week of George Bernard Shaw's "Man and Superman" at the Community Playhouse. The play is the first to have extended run over the old schedule of twelve performances, and attendance has held up very well. The daring and original abstract constructionist settings by Ralph Scarlett have been the occasion of much discussion. But on the whole it has been both encouraging and a little surprising how general has been the acceptance by the public of the new franchise that gives the artist the right to experiment with any means that may reach and reveal that "deeper reality that lies beyond realism."

The psycho-analysts have blazed the way. Strange doings, we have discovered, go on under the everyday traffic of man's conventionalized give-and-take of social intercourse. The modern artist is almost as much concerned with laboratory analysis as the astro-phyicist. And the purpose is the same: a new knowledge and understanding of the light that lightens our darkness to a new day.

Dream Scene Given

What is sometimes called the dream scene, sometimes, the hell scene, or the Don Juan scene, in the third act of "Man and Superman," because of its tremendous exactions both on audience and players, is seldom given stage presentation. Gilmor Brown stepped before the curtain Monday night to explain that for these reasons it was presented only twice (at the two Monday performances) in the Playhouse production. He warned his hearers that the average audience would probably be happier without it; and he said that anyone who wished to get home before 12 o'clock could go to the box office and change tickets for another evening. Evidently nobody was "average," since so far as I could learn no one took advantage of this offer.

Performance Pleases

In this scene again, Ralph Scarlett's abstract expressionistic settings elucidate the meaning and bridge technical difficulties of costume change and scene shift. Practically Harrison Ford in the role of Don Juan is the sole protagonist. Lighted masks lifted one above the other in a triptych of portraitlike panels take the place of the devil, the statue and Ana. The off-stage voices of Norvall Mitchell, Ralph Freud, and Florence Mason, serve to identify these parts. It is as tricky and difficult a bit of modern stage symbolism as I have ever seen executed. And last night's presentation was vastly to the credit of all concerned. In particular one must salute Harrison Ford for his brilliant and splendidly sustained performance. It is to be accounted a veritable tour de force. Mr. Ford came through the ordeal with flying colors.

As the play has already received extended notice in these columns, I will add only the rather interesting analysis of Mr. Scarlett's production: The first act contains twenty individual parts of scenery, five property pieces and eleven red "spikes" that serve to emotionalize the light plot. The second act has nine scenic pieces, five bits of property, and the eleven spikes. The third act, ten scene-building bits and three properties, and the fourth act, nine pieces for background construction and five properties. The red spikes are differently built into each of these scenes. "Man and Superman" will run till the end of this week, with Saturday matinee as usual. I can only repeat it is one of the most significant and stimulating productions the Community Playhouse has ever staged.

REALISM OR ABSTRACTION?

FEBRUARY 9, 1930

Weston's Photographs and Scarlett's Paintings Offer Timely Aid to Understanding of Art

BY ARTHUR MILLIER

Since we are committed to a series of biweekly Wednesday morning talks about the bases of art creation and appreciation, we are naturally on the lookout for helpful material. In two exhibition, that of photographs by Edward Weston at the Braxton Galleries this month, and the showing of abstract paintings by Rolph Scarlett at the Hagemeyer studio, Pasadena, during this week, the student of art will find a useful and enjoyable lesson.

Several panygerics on Weston's photographs have been printed in these columns during the last four years, exhausting our stock of adjectives. We believe that the work and the influence of this photographer will be written large in the history of art in the West and in America. Rolph Scarlett is a newcomer, his first impression on the public being the sets for the Pasadena Community Playhouse production of "Man and Superman," which are said to have been daringly effective.

But the point of interest in these showings appearing simultaneously is that each man approaches nature from an exactly opposite angle to result in something that can only be called art if it is properly grasped. At Braxton's we see Weston sharpening the single eye of his camera to exact from nature the minutest details barely visible to the human eye. His approach to art is by way of absolute realism, realism such as should commend itself to the most hide-bound academician.

PUZZLES OR PICTURES?

Scarlett takes the opposite point of departure. Out of two galleries full of paintings in oils and water colors it is difficult to discover what material things serve as the bases of these bewilderingly brilliant designs. Perhaps a day given to the task might resolve most of these puzzles to their realistic ingredients. Here is one patently designed from the elements of a camera. A large oil seems to be made up of parts found in an auto repair shop, another has forms from a metal foundry, and another clearly contains copper pots.

REALISM TO ABSTRACT

Now the academic-minded fail to enjoy Weston's prints to the full because his absolute realism seems to them to be abstract. He discovers that the simplest objects have rare forms to ravish the sensitive eye. He finds remarkable combinations of form that do not, at first, tally with the obvious view of nature. Even in his portraits we see the individual apparently invested with a grandeur of form that is unfamiliar. But nature and a sharp lens do it all for him. The genius consists here, as anywhere, in realizing what beauty there is in nature.

But our academician would be equally scandalized by the liberties Rolph Scarlett takes with forms. He follows the familiar practice of the Frenchmen who break up common forms and recombine them into new patterns. This sort of thing is taught as an exercise in art schools today but the result is usually cold and mechanical. Not so the abstractions of Rolph Scarlett. They are warm and moving, charming to the eye by their movement, shape and color, and infinitely varied. No two are alike. If any artist thinks it is easy let him try it.

POTS OR PEPPERS

Fundamentally that is the business of the artist, combining forms and colors. And whether he does it like Weston, by setting up two peppers or two shells in some charming relation to each other so that they delight the eye and stir the imagination; or whether, like Scarlett, he takes springs, sheets of corrugated iron, circles or brass strips, and, in the heat of his imagination, causes these things to dance into new patterns; or whether he takes some traditional form of landscape or portrait and invigorates it with new life, there will be nothing vital come of his activity if the forms and colors are not beautiful and well related, apart from their meaning as things in nature. We repeat, these two exhibitions, taken together, offer a welcome course in the simple elements of art.

HOMAGE TO HILLA REBAY

Excerpted from the catalog for the exhibition Homage to Hilla Rebay *at the Carlson Gallery, University of Bridgeport, 1972, by Bruce Glaser, Director of Exhibition.*

Hilla Rebay belonged to the great tradition of modern art that has declared many times over in the past one hundred twenty-five years that the formal properties of a work of art rather than any representational subject is its true content. And it might be added, that she said it more uncompromisingly than anybody else. For comparison, Maurice Denis' classic statement, virtually memorized by every student of modern art ("a picture before being a horse, a nude, or an anecdote — is essentially a flat surface covered with colors assembled in a certain order"), did not call for the elimination of subject matter, let alone declare that representational work was inferior. But a group of artists in the early part of our century, of which Hilla Rebay was one and Vasily Kandinsky the primal figure, extended such insights of the previous century to their logical conclusion. Kandinsky in an early autobiography published in German in 1912 was the first to apply the term "non-objective" in reference to several of his paintings which he called "Gegenstandslos" (literally, without object). It was Kandinsky, also, who must be traced as the source for both the equation between spirituality and non-objective art, and the analogy between music and non-objective art which Hilla Rebay vigorously promoted in her own writings, lectures and through her editing and translations of Kandinsky's key essays.

Miss Rebay's interpretations of these ideas, however, were characteristically homiletic and didactic, geared as they were to a resistant and suspicious public. She would not even compromise her ideas with those who might be partially sympathetic to her goals as when she extended her castigation of representational art to abstract art as well. Abstraction, she believed, was simply a reduction of details of objects as they exist in nature, while non-objective art was created independently, from its inception, in the fashion of musical composition. In non-objective art, one would strive to exorcise any resemblance to known objects or their associative qualities. Thus, it was reasoned, one would be aware of the higher spiritual qualities of the work rather than of a possible functional role such as illustration.

One has the sense in reading Hilla Rebay's essays that individual sentences were meant to be isolated from their context and to stand as incontrovertible aphorisms:

"The purity of space on a virgin canvas is already ruined by an objective beginning".

"The Non-Objective picture is far superior to all others in its influential potentiality, educational power, and spiritual value to humanity".

"Those who oppose Non-Objectivity have not as yet experienced its uplifting wealth".

The force and implied commitment of these statements is a reverberation of Hilla Rebay's personality which has been recalled as powerful, honest and earthy. One did not generally come away from her with a vague feeling. One believed in her or avoided her.

Her role as Curator and Director of the Museum of Non-Objective Painting in New York, now the Solomon R. Guggenheim Museum, was a vocation and her vision of the museum was that of a temple sanctified by its purpose and its contents. When she wrote, "The rare art collection of the [Solomon R. Guggenheim] Foundation creates a center of spiritual power" she evoked the ancient and primitive concept of art as a real and effective factor in the lives of men and not as the precious, elitist commodity that it has so often become. The unfortunate fact is that a relatively small public took advantage of the exhibitions at the Museum of Non-Objective Art, or even understood the seriousness of the venture.

However, a number of young American artists were very appreciative of this luxury which allowed them to see vanguard art at a time when it was rarely exhibited in other museums or galleries.

There were too few occasions in the formative years of the museum when the public, rather than just artists, came in large numbers. Once, in 1939, they came to see the kinds of paintings that were said to have inspired the symbol of the New York World's Fair, the Trylon and Perisphere. The Bauers and Kandinskys filled with circles and triangles were associated with a popular symbol of the future and therefore they finally could be digested.

The cultural climate in New York had matured during World War II. Part of the reason for this lay in the inaccessibility of the art centers of Europe at that time and the flight to America of a significant group of vanguard artists and writers.

But part of the reason also lay in the return on the investment in exhibitions, ideas and patronage to which Hilla Rebay devoted herself. And it is well documented that enterprise such as hers, along with the pioneer work of other men and women who persistently advocated the new art, had helped prepare the soil for the extraordinary efflorescence of post-war American art.

Inside Art | Carol Vogel

- Early Guggenheim purchases for sale
- Art as collateral on the rise
- Mid-priced buyers seem to be back.

Out of the Guggenheim's Core

Is the Solomon R. Guggenheim Museum selling off its history?

The museum's curators don't think so. But Gary Snyder, owner of Snyder Fine Art, a gallery on West 57th Street in Manhattan, is happily capitalizing on their actions, however they are defined.

Mr. Snyder's current show, "The Museum of Non-Objective Painting, American Abstract Art," which is on view at 20 West 57th Street through May 11, features work by artists like Rolph Scarlett, Rudolf Bauer and Hilla Rebay from the 1930's and 40's.

Their work formed the core of the Museum of Non-Objective Painting, which opened in 1939 at 24 East 54th Street to showcase Mr. Guggenheim's collection of abstract art and was the forerunner of the Guggenheim Museum, which opened in 1959.

More than half of the 28 paintings and works on paper in Mr. Snyder's show are from the Guggenheim's original collection. Many were sold by the museum to Steve Lowy, a private dealer in Manhattan, over the last decade. Mr. Lowy has put them in Mr. Snyder's show on consignment.

For a museum to sell art privately rather than at public auction is unusual. To avoid conflicts of interest and criticism, most institutions decide to sell their art in a public arena.

"We've deaccessioned both publicly and privately," said Lisa Dennison, a curator at the Guggenheim. "The museum was approached by a dealer who said there was tremendous interest in these works, so we examined our holdings. We also spoke to both Sotheby's and Christie's but felt that selling privately would be more lucrative."

Mr. Lowy declined to comment on his dealings with the Guggenheim, saying that the transactions he makes with his clients are confidential.

Ms. Dennison would not specify how much money the museum made from the sale of the paintings, but she said that the Guggenheim sold 24 works in a group and that the money was put into a fund for art purchases.

Mr. Snyder, noting that the market for this kind of art is growing, said 14 works from his current show had been sold.

He added that he believed the Guggenheim officials who decided what works the museum would sell might "not have the best eye."

"To let go of a Scarlett like this," he said, referring to "Composition," a colorful painting from 1938-39, "is to ignore the roots of Abstract Expressionism. But they don't consider this historical period to be of any value. They don't think this stuff can compete with Abstract Expressionists or European modernism."

"In every case, we still have huge holdings by these artists," Ms. Dennison said. "We are not overlooking our history."

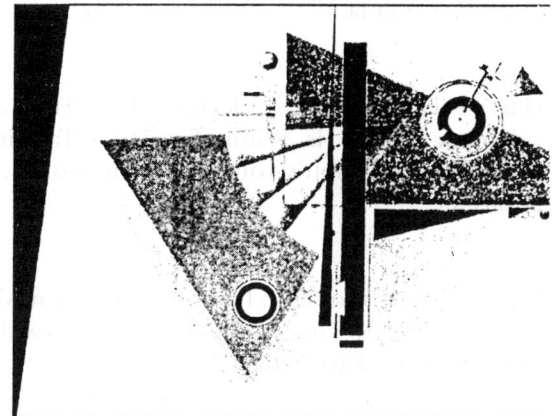

Rolph Scarlett's "Composition," once owned by the Guggenheim

Sale of Scarlett's painting, *Composition*, by a private dealer; this was the first Scarlett work bought by Solo.non R. Guggenheim for his collection.

CREDITS

Chronology by Harriet Tannin, Executor, Rolph Scarlett Estate, and Judith Nasby, Director, MacDonald Stewart Art Center, The University of Guelph, Ontario, Canada.

Harriet Tannin with camerman Tom Hull also produced a 20-minute videotape, "Who is Rolph Scarlett." Tannin serves as interviewer to prod Rolph Scarlett's voluminous memories. Tape is available from the publisher.

Front cover, left to right: Irene Guggenheim, Vasily Kandinsky, Hilla Rebay, and Solomon R. Guggenheim, July 1930, with Museum of Non-objective Painting in background.

Back cover: Elliott Barowitz, *Yellow Cady in front of the Gugg*, 40 x 50 in.